Blue Skies & Tail Winds

LITTLE SLICE OF HEAVEN

To T.J.
From, Lowell Farrand

Lowell Farrand

Hope you Enjoy

As told to Rebecca McLendon

Because You are my help,
I sing in the shadow of Your
wings.

Psalm 63:7

DEDICATION

I would like to dedicate this book to my wife, Gaylia and our sons, Grant and Jim, their families and all the kids who have blessed our lives through the years. Also, a special thanks to all the plane dealers and FBOs who influenced my life.

INTRODUCTION

"May the favor of the Lord our God rest upon us,
establish the work of our hands for us—yes establish the
work of our hands." Psalm 90:17

I was born with my right arm going behind me instead of in front of me. At the same time, a baby girl was born with the same condition as mine. Strangely enough, our mothers were very best friends. Mom's doctor said they could try a series of breaks and each time bring the arm closer to normal. He thought it would take about five surgeries. The girl's doctor, however, told her mother that kind of treatment would be too cruel for a baby to stand. He thought they should wait until she was ten, and then break it and re-set it.

My doctor broke my arm the five times to get it around to normal. My sister says that when I was little, my arm was always in a cast, but my arm grew normally along with the rest of my body, with the exception of the two bones from my elbow to my wrist, which had grown together from being in the cast so long. As a result, my right arm would not turn or swivel. I couldn't use a screwdriver with my right arm, but I still could do my work OK.

When I was 27 years old, I was carrying a large console TV down a steep stairway with a customer. He dropped his end, leaving all the weight on me. My right arm snapped so loudly I could hear it. It hurt so badly, I was sure I had broken it. I went to the doctor immediately, and he took x-rays and came out laughing.

"What's so funny about a broken arm?" I asked.

He said, "It's not broken! The two bones that had been grown together had just snapped apart, and after this heals, you will be normal and able to use a screwdriver in either hand!"

The doctor of the little girl had waited until she was ten years old and broke her arm and moved it to the front. After it healed, it never grew any more. As her body grew, the arm stayed the same small size and wasn't very useful. However, she grew up, married, had a family and worked as a bank teller for many years. I am so glad that my doctor made the choices that he did.

Since my right arm had been so long in healing, I was naturally left-handed. The teachers at school insisted that I write with my right hand. That is what they thought they were supposed to do, and they spent much time trying to correct those left-handed pupils. I did learn to write with my right hand, but it wasn't comfortable. When my teacher again insisted that I write with my right hand, I would tell her, "All people were born left-handed, and then some of you sinned!" This made her so mad that she turned red! We never got along very well.

Now that I am older, I wish I had kept writing with my right hand, too. After graduating from school, I didn't have to, so I gradually lost the ability.

EARLY YEARS

My earliest memory puts me sitting on boxes in the back seat of my dad's old Model A Ford. We were moving from east of Goshen, Indiana, to the place that we would later call "the Home Place. According to my Mom, I was only three years old, but I clearly remember the sandy, hilly road that we "kinda got stuck in."

I do not remember anything else until my first day of school. There was no kindergarten then, so I began my education in the First Grade. The bus driver lived at the other end of Zollinger Road, and our road "T-d" into it. The bus driver told all of us kids on my road to walk down to the T to be picked up. It was one mile. In the "T" lay Alderman lake on the other side of the fence. Little did I know that this lake was going to be a part of my life later on.

Each afternoon, the school bus driver would let all of us off at the "T," so we had to walk that same mile back to our homes. To make matters worse, the older boys made us pay a penny to get past them, or they would beat us up. Once I didn't have a penny, and I arrived home bruised, and my clothes were torn. Dad took off his belt and beat me. I didn't understand why.

"Every time you come home like this and have lost a fight, you'll get a good 'lickin'," he said, "until you learn to stand up for yourself."

"But they're bigger than me!" I protested.

"Hit first, and hardest, then you won't have to worry about the rest."

So, I decided then and there, that I would become the meanest, toughest kid around. I learned that I wanted to be alone. I didn't like people at that point. When I got off the bus each day, I crawled through the fence and went to play in Alderman Lake until all the other kids got home. Mom said I never came home until I had fallen in that lake and gotten wet. I even did this in the wintertime and walked home many times with my pants legs frozen stiff.

THE OLD HOME PLACE

Our home place was too small to make a living at farming. Originally, there was enough land to farm, but Mom almost died when I was born, so Dad had to sell a lot of land to pay the hospital bill. Dad had to work at a factory to make ends meet.

We had just enough land to grow some corn, hay and some wheat to feed our animals—two cows for milk, two sows and a litter of pigs, ten chickens, my turtle, George, my pigeon, Pal and my dog, Shep. My sister Caroline made dress clothes for the piglets. She dressed them and pushed them around in a wicker baby buggy. Those piglets would lie in your arms just like a baby. I don't think they knew they were supposed to be pigs. In addition to the piglets, Caroline dressed some of the baby chicks when they were little. It's a miracle they survived all that attention!

One night, my sister and her girlfriend wanted to sleep in our tent. It was a nice tent—almost six feet high in the center with four-foot walls. There was an army cot on each side. After I saw they were fast asleep, I brought Rose, the cow into the tent and tied her halter to the tent pole and snuck out! A little later, the girls woke up, screaming bloody murder! Their screams scared the cow, and the tent came down on top of the cow, who was now running around in circles with a tent on her head! The girls went inside the house to sleep, and then I got into REAL trouble! Mom spanked me hard with a willow switch, and the next morning she made me put the tent back up.

Pal, my pet pigeon came to me when a storm blew his nest down, and I rescued him. Apparently, his mother abandoned him. He was just a baby, and I fed him. He grew up sitting on my shoulder and went everywhere with me. Even when I rode my bicycle, Pal would sit on my shoulder, grabbing my ear lobe with his beak to hold on. He even went on my paper route with me. He seemed to know the route as well as I did. He would often fly ahead to the next house and wait for me. He knew which houses got the paper—a very smart bird. He was also smart enough to know the difference between boys and girls.

As I grew up and worked away from home and was planning the wedding with Gay, Pal apparently felt he was not getting enough attention and left. I think he must have found a girlfriend, too. Several years later, as I was working outside my TV shop just across the road from my parents' "Old Home Place," a pigeon came and landed on my shoulder, squawking excessively. I reached up to pet him, but he flew away. I always thought it was Pal.

George the turtle always got along with Pal. My dog Shep seemed to think it was his job to look after both of them. It was strange how Rose, the cow and the turtle also bonded. George always wanted to sleep with Rose at night, and, when it got dark, if George wasn't in the barn, Rose would look all over the place for him. I think a cow and a turtle make "strange bedfellows!"

For a few years, Shep and I had muskrat traps at a large pond. Every morning, we would check the traps before school. One morning, we had a skunk in the trap. Consequently, Mom gave both Shep and me baths in tomato juice. However, when I got to school, I was sent home immediately. For two days Mom almost scrubbed my skin off.

That pond, filled with great adventures for Shep and me, has now become a golf course.

SLEEP WALKING

When I was about seven years old, I fell to sleep-walking. My concerned parents took me to a number of doctors who told them, "Oh, he'll grow out of it." They were right—I did eventually stop. During those years, however, I think I just about drove my folks crazy!

I slept upstairs in our house and would get up, go downstairs in my pajamas, go outside and start my dad's tractor. I plowed and cultivated the corn, even though I was sound asleep! I didn't plow out any corn, except at the ends where I turned around! Even though I was only seven when I started this, I was very strong when I was sleepwalking.

I could push Dad away, and it scared the heck out of Mom.

"He must be a zombie or something!" they would say.

Being poor, we couldn't afford a regular tractor, so Dad bought an old junk Dodge truck for $35. We dragged it home, and Dad took the body off and cut the truck down short. He installed two transmissions, back to back, to gear it down like a tractor. He made the controls so that a person could either stand up or sit down to drive it. I could stand up and drive it quite well.

When I went sleep walking, however, I would go right for the tractor which we called "Our Whoopie." Dad fixed the fuel valve so he thought that I couldn't find it, but I always found it, even in my sleep, and plowed more corn!

The folks tied rope across the stairway with bells on it, put extra locks on the doors, and fixed the tractor so that it wouldn't run. But somehow I got out of the house anyway.

"He must have walked right through the doors. They were still locked!"

Since the tractor wouldn't run, I got my bike and rode down to the lake. Dad finally found me sitting on the pier in my pajamas with my feet dangling in the water. He slapped me awake, but I couldn't remember anything about how I ended up at the lake.

The folks were going "nuts"! They had tried pills, extra locks on the doors, ropes and bells across the stairs and disabling the tractor, and hiding my bike. Finally, at age nine, I stopped sleepwalking and never did it again!

THE OLD HERMIT

At the lake there was a large pier where an old hermit lived in a tar paper shack. He rented old wooden boats and sold bait. He had a beard down to his waist and never shaved. Everyone was scared of him. They all said he was very bad, and told Mom that he might do bad things to me and maybe even kill me! But all he did was sit on the pier and tell me stories. He became my friend. I sat and listened to many stories over the years.

One morning, when I was ten years old, I was eating breakfast—you know, those big shredded wheat. biscuits—when the house and ground outside began to shake. All the neighbors started yelling, "EARTHQUAKE! EARTHQUAKE!" But then someone said, "No! Earthquakes only last a few minutes, but this is going on and on and ON." The men had already left for work, so all of us went out to the road and saw all the other women and children. We gathered together in a huddle. Many of the women were crying, and others were praying.

"The world is coming to an end! This is the END!" The shaking and the roar got louder and louder. The police and firemen were following the roar and it led them to the lake. While everyone was so sure the world was coming to an end, I ran down to the pier where the old hermit calmly sat there.

"What's happening?" I hollered.

"Oh, just the lake going dry. It's happened before. My grandpappy told me this had happened before, but this is the first time I've gotten to see it.

"Ya see, son, there are caverns under here and also an underground river. The lake bottom has just broken through. It takes fifteen to twenty feet of silt to hold the lake bottom, but the tides and the moon wash it back and forth every evening. Finally it will break through the caverns underneath and the lake goes dry. Reeds weeds, and bushes grow up and die down which starts the process of making more silt. This takes forty years coming and forty years going!"

Everyone said he was nuts, and I was crazy for listening to that. That evening most of the town turned out with washtubs and dishpans to pick up all the fish they could carry. I found a snapping turtle with about a two-foot diameter shell and dragged home with my belt. I didn't realize snapping turtles can snap off a hand. He was my pet for over two years. I kept him in a sunken tub filled with water in the back yard. In the winter I put him in the barn. He liked sleeping under the cows in the hay. One spring morning he was gone, I always hoped he made it back to the swamp where the lake had been.

One day I sat on the pier with the old hermit and said, "I don't like people, but why don't *you* like people?"

"Oh! I like people!" he answered. "I just don't want them running my life."

He continued, "I had a big office in Chicago and ran a big company. One day, I just walked out and never looked back. My grandpappy had owned all the property around this lake, and when he died, it all became mine. I came here and found everything I needed—right here!"

I had heard folks talking about how the oil company had given him lot of money for the oil rights. He went right out and bought a new car and parked it beside the tar paper shack. I never saw him drive it, but I got to sit in it and pretend I was driving it. One day, however, I went to see him, but the car was gone, and so was he. I did keep playing in the tar paper shack, hoping that maybe someday he might come back. He never did. Now I regularly fly over the lake and the spot where the shack had been. It brings a lot of good old memories flooding back.

THE CELERY MARSH

Purdue University came to do a study of the lake and took soundings which proved the hermit was exactly correct in what he said about it. There were indeed caverns under it with an underground river flowing south to the Celery Marsh. The pressure of the water pushed the Celery Marsh up and flooded it, making it totally unusable.

I hated to see this, because my first job at the age of ten was planting celery. The neighbor lady told Mom she shouldn't let me work at that young age, but I loved the work and got thirty-five cents a day! I was able to buy a used bike with my earnings.

The muck ground was so soft that you couldn't use machinery because they would sink in. We used horses with special wooden shoes. Everybody said I was that crazy kid who talked about putting wooden shoes on horses.

They laughed at me, "How could you put wooden shoes on horses?"

The horses, however, were so well-trained they would hold up a foot while you put the shoe on or took it off. I'd hug them around the neck and tell them what we were going to do. They seemed to understand and waited patiently until they had four shoes.

The Celery Marsh got its name back when the Big 4 Railroad ended at Goshen, Indiana. The Hollanders left their homeland because of religious persecution and had taken the train as far West as it could take them. They got off the train in Goshen and noticed the swamp ground in East Goshen could be purchased for almost nothing. Being from Holland, they understood how to drain the land, and they started growing celery just like they did in their homeland. They carved wooden shoes for the horses to spread the load of their hooves, so they wouldn't sink in. They sold their celery from wagons to all the towns and cities around. They had big greenhouses where they grew the plants, and also the big tanks in which to wash the celery.

I planted row after row of celery by making a hole with a stick and putting the tiny plants in the holes. I really loved working with the horses, even though I was "that crazy kid." Many years later, just recently in fact, our local Historical Society presented a program to a large group of people about the Hollanders settling in Goshen, draining the land and planting celery. They used horses equipped with wooden shoes to pull the cart with a person planting the seedlings. They made quite a story about how the Hollanders made the wooden shoes for their horses.

The program speaker, who happened to be a high school friend of mine, came up to me and said, "NOW, maybe somebody will believe us about those wooden shoes on our horses!"

It turns out the speaker was a descendent of one of those settlers.

My wife Gay and I happened to drive through that area not long ago. It's still too wet to farm. Reeds and bushes are about five feet tall. The city had made some of the land into a neighborhood nature/playground park. After each winter the reeds and bushes die down, creating a base for the ground—before long it might support farming again. It has been about seventy years.

Back when Purdue was doing a study and taking drilling samples, they found oil. Standard Oil came to investigate and said at the time there was not enough to make it profitable; however, they wanted to buy the oil rights in case they ever needed it.

Folks talked about how the oil company had given him lot of money for the oil rights. He went right out and bought a new car and parked it beside the tar paper shack. I never saw him drive it, but I got to sit in it and pretend I was driving it. One day, however, I went to see him, but the car was gone, and so was he. I did keep playing in the tar paper shack, hoping that maybe someday he might come back. He never did.

I recently took my Luscombe up and flew over the old Celery Marsh and the lake. Memories of the old pier, the crazy old hermit, and this crazy kid bring tears to my eyes.

The lake is now about half full. If you look at the shoreline of what us kids called the "drop off," it will have to rise another twelve to fifteen feet to reach its original shoreline. From the air I can see some beautiful, expensive homes lower down, closer to where the shoreline is now. IF that lake comes back to its original depth—they may be in trouble.

EARLY JOBS AND THEIR REWARDS

I joined the Boy Scouts when I was twelve years old. My uncle Ed was Scoutmaster of Troop 23 which met at St. Mark's Methodist Church. Our troop was scheduled to host a Jamboree at the Elkhart County Fairgrounds. This included the troops from northern Indiana. My uncle wanted us to serve a pancake breakfast for all the troops and their parents, which would be quite an undertaking.

The local stores and businesses were very generous with donations to help us with the breakfast. Thanks to the A & P store, we got many sacks of pancake mix. The hardware store furnished a brand new cement mixer to mix the batter and new shovels to scoop out shovel sized pancakes. The Goshen Iron and Metal donated a 4 x 8 foot steel plate for a griddle, and the propane company furnished four burners to heat the steel plate. Local farmers donated gallons of maple syrup and homemade apple butter. We served pancakes all day long, and everyone said it was the best Jamboree ever!

My cousin, Rollin Farrand, worked at Kline's Department Store in the Men's Department. He got me a job there as soon as I turned thirteen. At that time, you had to be thirteen in order to get a job at a store in Goshen. My job as stock boy was to stock shelves, clean and sweep the floor. After I had been there a good while, the assistant manager gave me a white shirt, a tie and a sweater.

"We will tell you a day ahead of time when to dress up. Be sure your tie is tied "just so" and that your shoes are polished."

That day finally came, and I sensed that there was something "big" going on at Kline's. Everybody was wearing their very best. A big black limo stopped at the back door. Several body guards dressed in black suits surrounded the limo, and a lady got out and was rushed into the freight elevator. One of the men told me I was to take her to the top floor. A ladies sitting room decorated with all the "feminine frills" was located on the top floor. I was expected to keep the ladies in coffee, tea and doughnuts.

Every time I served the lady from the limo, she kissed me on the cheek. As a kid, I was kind of embarrassed.

"It is a custom in her country," someone whispered to me.

It turns out that this important lady was Golda Mier, who would later become Prime Minister of Israel. The Kline's Department Store was owned by Mr. Katzinger, who was married to Golda Mier's sister. Golda came every few months to visit her sister.

While waiting on her to finish her visit, I spent time with the body guards. Since I was interested in cars, they showed me the limo. It was completely bullet proof all around—even the tires. They also showed me their shoulder holsters. As a thirteen year old, I was really impressed. We did this about four times a year.

I bet I am the only man alive that had been kissed on the cheek so many times by Golda Meir, the Prime Minister of Israel.

THE HAND CAR INCIDENT

Back when I was about ten or twelve, there was a railroad track which came up from the South through East Goshen, heading north through farm land, over to Middlebury and then northeast to Stone Lake and on to Burr Oak, Michigan. While growing up on Hackett Road, I would ride my bike east on the gravel road to where the track crossed it and headed toward Stone Lake. I noticed at the crossing there was a hand pump rail car sitting beside the track. I got a couple of kids to help and see if we could get the car up on the track.

We did, and we started to pump the car north through the woods. We were amazed how beautiful the woods were and how many wild animals we saw. We made several short runs through those woods. One time we decided to do it at night so we could see the animals' eyes. It was kind of scary but neat!

As summer came on, I said to my "buddies," "Hey! I think we could take this thing all the way to Stone Lake and go swimming!"

So, we did just that—many times during that summer. However, one day we swam a lot longer than we thought. It was getting late, so we hurried up and started home through the woods. We were pumping fast and furious and had lots of speed built up. This particular old rail car had a big fly wheel. Once you got it up to speed, it took a long time to stop. As we came around a bend in the woods we saw a train coming toward us. We all bailed off that hand car and ran as fast as we could, considering we were limping from jumping down so hard. We ran into the woods and suddenly heard a big crash. We knew what it was and kept running, never looking back! We had a long walk back home.

Later some men came asking questions about the hand car, and who was on it. Of course, us kids "didn't know nuthin' about any hand car! Many years have passed, and the railroad tracks are gone. The park department has made a blacktopped hiking/jogging path out of the rail bed.

Railroad Hand Car

Lowell Farrand

HIGH SCHOOL: TALKIN' 'BOUT CHROME-PLATED FANTASIES AND MY GIRL GAY

While growing up I was kind of a "loner." I didn't really like people and didn't get along very well in school. Even at six years of age I was thinking about airplanes, drawing model airplane plans and building balsa wood models. I couldn't see why I needed all that "school stuff". I purposely got into trouble so I would get "kicked out of school." I would then go home and work on model airplanes. I was kicked out more than any other kid there.

A lot of times I would ride my bike to the airport hoping to see an airplane fly. I started washing the airplanes to get a quick ride around the field. This continued until I was about fourteen. By then, I was washing the airplanes and taking them around the field to "air dry" them. Between the ages of fourteen and seventeen, I was riding with students to teach them crosswind landings, even though I didn't have a pilot license.

By this time I was also getting interested in cars.. I bought a $50-dollar car to rebuild. At that time, if you were taking the auto mechanics class in high school, you were allowed to work afternoons at one of the local garages. I worked at the local Olds/Cadillac dealership Mondays through Fridays, and then on Saturdays I went with my friend Rich to work at his uncle's electrical business.

Although I had noticed the little blonde girl in Sunday School for several years, it wasn't until our MYF (Youth Group) had a hayride that I thought I needed to get to know Gay better. I was older then, and the hormones must have kicked in. My friend "Uppie" and I didn't have dates, so we tagged behind the wagon and teased Gay and her date and several other couples. I never let up on the teasing, and I slipped her notes later at school. We eventually started attending school events and ball games together. We walked home from the games and movies and usually stopped at the Coffee Cup Restaurant or the Olympia Candy Kitchen for Vanilla Cokes, Green Rivers, Phosphates and the best sodas imaginable! After we started going to the movies, we called them "real dates!"

Several years later, when we were seniors in High School, our MYF had a paper drive where people put their old newspapers on their front porches for us to pick up. One of the houses had a jewelry store in the front called Luke's. I asked Gay if she would like to pick out a ring! She said, "Sure!"

That was her eighteenth birthday gift, and she's worn that ring for 67 years, and still has me too!

My high school days didn't go any better than my grade school, as far as teachers were concerned. I was just not very good with them. However, there were two that I really liked. Mr. Sabin taught Agriculture and kept Study Hall. He was a very large man. No matter how bad I was, he would put his arm around me and treated me like a son. I respected him and kept in touch with him after I graduated.

My Auto Mechanics teacher, "Pop" Kintigh, was also very well loved by all the boys. He could have come down on me very hard, but he never did. In his class we would choose a car motor on a test stand and took it apart—every piece. We had to get it to where we could put it back together, start it up and then tune it up. I chose the biggest engine—a Buick Century straight 8. We had flex exhaust hoses and a ventilator suction tube. I noticed that the heating register was next to our exhaust tube. I knew Gay was in her art class in the room above us, so I switched the tubes, poured oil into the engine that I was running! It filled up the art room with smoke!

Needless to say, Mr. Sprunger, the Art teacher was really ranting and raving, as he entered the Mechanics shop.

"I want the kid responsible for that smoke expelled!"

"Pop" told him, "Go back to your classroom. I'll take care of this."

I know that "Pop" knew that I was the culprit, but he looked at the class and said, "Listen now, boys. THIS IS NEVER GOING TO HAPPEN AGAIN! IS THAT CLEAR?"

We all hung our heads and said, "Yessir!"

He never singled me out, but we all knew, when he spoke, you listened!

Sadly, "Pop" died when I was a junior in high school. His son Max filled in for the remainder of my high school days. After graduation I worked for Max in his garage for a number of years.

I escaped expulsion from school with the smoke incident, but, on another occasion, a rich kid got to bragging about the new car his dad had bought him for his birthday. It was a brand-new tiny little Crosley! Us poorer kids got tired of his bragging, so we got together and carried it up to the third floor of the school. To this day, I cannot figure out how we accomplished that.

That afternoon in study hall, I felt a big hand on my shoulder, and the Principal said, "Lowell, you get that car down from the third floor, RIGHT NOW!"

Stupidly, I answered, "Why me? You don't know that I did it."

He leaned in and said, "Lowell, if there's a car on the third floor, I know you had something to do with it!"

It was a lot harder to take the car down than it was to get it up there! I was then expelled for the remainder of the day and the next one too!

Later, I got a real nice 1937 Buick Century with a "blown engine" for 50 bucks. I put in a junk yard engine and drove it for quite a while. When I was working at the Old/Cadillac place, I took Gay to see a V12 Cylinder 1937 LaSalle hearse that I wanted to buy. Oh, how I loved that twelve-cylinder engine. Besides, I thought that hearse was a real beauty. Surely Gay would love it too. However, as we sat in the thing, I heard Gay's voice from the very back of the hearse, which was about eight feet away.

"You are NOT getting this car! I am NOT riding in a HEARSE!"

That was that. I settled on a shiny black and chrome 1946 Buick Super with another "blown engine!" I got another junk yard engine for the car, and we drove that car on our honeymoon!

CLASS OF '51! OHHHH! *THAT* CLASS!

We were the only high school class where the whole class was expelled just before graduation! Even today, when people ask us what class we were in, we say, "The Class of '51." It never fails. They say "Ohhhh! *THAT* Class!"

Our Senior class had planned a "Senior Skip Day" to Pokagon State Park for a picnic and swimming. A young guy and a young lady teacher agreed to be our class sponsors. Both were very "cool" teachers. In fact the lady was a "hot car" buff.

The day started with us leaving the high school in each of our cars. Three of us boys ran around together, and we each had the 1938 coupes. Mine was a '38 Desoto. Rich had a '38 Plymouth Coupe, and Gene had a '38 Chevy Coupe. They were all black with chrome. We had all had an afterschool job at ARTCO Plating Co., where we had been plating those spiffy 1940's "modern" chrome kitchen tables and chairs. After midnight, however, we would plate anything that

43

could come loose from our cars. We had the best chrome in town! Most of our trips and lots of our dates involved going to junk yards in Indiana and Michigan looking for car parts for whatever rebuild we were working on at the time. The cars all had bench seats and center floor shifts. Gay was always with me—no matter whose car we took. She always sat in the center and did the shifting. Gay never missed a gear.

On the way to the Senior Skip, our lady sponsor passed me. I saw the grin on her face, so I passed her! We did this a number of times on the one hour drive to the park, and we arrived at the park entrance side by side. I saw the look on her face and put the pedal to the metal! It wasn't long before we were doing 102 mph, and she was right beside me. Well, I wasn't going to let a woman teacher beat me. We entered the parking lot and went into a big sliding turn. Luckily, we didn't hit anyone or anything.

The two sponsors and our three cars were all parked side by side, and everyone was having a great time picnicking and swimming. My two buddies and I snuck out to the parking lot and put tire smoke bombs on the sponsors' cars. We also put some smoke bombs on the spark plugs, plus some Limburger cheese on the manifolds. It wasn't long until we saw the sponsors run down to the beach, clothes and all, and dive into the water. They came up at the float.

The "rich and popular kids" had taken liquor and beer to the float. Some of the girls were really drunk and lost the tops of their swim suits because the boys had thrown the tops into the lake. Some of them were even throwing up, which was quite "yucko." The sponsors threw them into their cars.

I told my buddies and Gay, "Let's get outta here! When they start up those cars, all H*#@s gonna break loose." Normally, the sponsors would have taken the joke OK, but on top of everything that was happening, there was bound to be trouble. The one-hour drive was not going to be good. By the time we arrived home, our parents already knew what had happened. We all got "grilled real good" as to what part did we have in all of this. Our folks couldn't believe that we hadn't even gone swimming.

The very next day, the Principal and the School Board said they were not going to have a graduation ceremony for our class, and everyone was being expelled! However, some parents with money and "influence" talked to them, and they decided on a "modified" graduation ceremony. Those who admitted to drinking, etc. received their diplomas "privately," and could not give the speeches that ordinarily are part of graduation. It was many years before a senior class cvould have a "Senior Sneak." I am not sure they even do that anymore.

So that's how the Class of '51 made history as *THAT* CLASS!

COYNE ELECTRICAL SCHOOL

After graduating from high school, my friend Rich's uncle offered to pay for our schooling at the Coyne Electrical School in Chicago, if we would come back and work for him after we graduated. The course included electrical house wiring, industrial mill wiring and more. Rich was a better student than I was. It was a struggle for me, but we both finished.

Rich and I took turns driving back and forth every weekend in our old cars. Our Moms cooked and baked food for us to take back with us since we didn't have enough money to eat out. Our room was on the fourth floor of the YMCA, and we weren't allowed to take food into our rooms. We parked right below our window and lowered a rope down from the fourth floor to the car and pulled our food, along with a gallon of milk up to our window. Once, however, while raising the gallon of milk, it came loose from the rope and spilled milk all over the top of the car. It was a huge mess.

The YWCA and the YMCA were connected by one large lobby. One evening the YMCA manager came to Rich and me.

"There are two girls visiting some other girls here and have stayed too late to be safe walking home in Chicago. Could you take them home for me? You are the only two boys here that I would trust to do that."

"But our car is only a coupe," we protested.

"That is better than them walking home alone," he insisted.

We agreed, and four of us crammed into the coupe, and we took the girls home. All went well.

One Friday night driving out of Chicago there was very heavy traffic. This was many years before the four to six lane highways and toll roads were built. Our right front wheel and brake assembly came off. I could hardly steer, but I managed to drive around several gas pumps and got it stopped. We were in East Chicago, and they told us the nearest junk yard that would have some old parts like we needed was in Hammond.

It was 5:00 pm, and the junk yard was closing, but we had just enough time for the dealer to use a torch and cut off the right front wheel assembly, brakes and all! We got it for five dollars—all the money Rich and I had. The assembly was heavy and we carried it between us while trying to run back to East Chicago. My foot slipped on a railroad track and hurt like thunder!

We did get back and fixed the car. We arrived home very late. Gay and my mom were sitting on the couch worrying about us being so late. It was also one of the worst winters ever, with lots of ice and snow. Our teacher at Coyne, knowing that we drove home on Friday nights, even in bad weather, told us to leave early on Fridays after that. We had to use tire chains all the way home. When we got to the big bridge in Chicago, the cars ahead of us couldn't get up the bridge, due to the ice. Since we had the tire chains on, we pushed the other cars across the bridge so we could head home. It was a rough winter, but we made it through the whole course and graduated.

As agreed, we returned to Rich's uncle's electrical business to work. Eventually he got hard to work for, so I quit and went back to the Olds/Cadillac dealership. I later found out that his uncle was sick and not feeling well. Soon after that, he passed away. I have always felt badly about quitting, because maybe I let him down when he needed me. I guess I wasn't grown up enough to really understand the situation.

ENGINES AND ELECTRONICS

The Oldsmobile Company had developed the Rocket 88 engine. Everyone seemed to have trouble starting it if it was still hot. It was a carburetor problem—more specifically, the Rochester carburetor. They sent me to school to learn how to fix that problem. It was the first time I really enjoyed school of any kind.

The Cadillacs seemed to have a similar problem, so they sent me to Carter Carb School where we learned to fix the same problem. Back at the garage, they put me on the tune up rack, which was a nice clean job. The older mechanics were very jealous of me, since they had been there for years, doing dirty, greasy work. Here I was "just a kid" and had a clean job. I loved the tune up rack and also learned to love engines.

The service manager, Max Kintigh, who had been our auto mechanics teacher after his father passed away, started his own garage, basically to service Olds's and Caddys. I went with him to do the tune ups. While working for Max, I also became interested in electronics and radio. TV was just beginning to be popular, so I started my own business on the side of selling and repairing TVs and radios.

Max even helped me install antennas. My business grew, which was exciting, so I built my own TV store and shop with the help of my uncle Ed. As the business grew, I hired a helper. I was now running the business full time, and business was good, but I had trouble collecting the payments. I loved the business, but Gay spent a lot of time on the road trying to collect payments. She was not happy.

Also at that time I was doing service work for Eisenhour Antenna Service. He approached me about combining the TV and Antenna business as a partnership. He would do all of the billing and collecting. The business was very successful. We made good money, but were working so many hours that the partnership became very stressful.

One day my doctor told me, "Lowell, if you don't quit that rat race, I will quit it for you!"

On New Year's Day we were taking inventory. I had worked almost 80 hours that week. I collapsed on the shop floor and ended up in the hospital. It was going to be a long recovery.

Our TV Business with my partner's VW service truck.

RECOVERY AND LIFE CHANGES

After I collapsed and my hospital stay, I was bedfast and not doing very well. I couldn't do my regular job, so my partner hired another fellow. I realized that we had to dissolve the partnership. My partner was always a great hunter, but the stress of the business caused him to have heart problems. The doctor recommended that he get away for a while. So he went to Montana hunting by himself. Later they found him lying beside his truck with a bottle of nitro pills in his hand.

As a result of this collapse, I was out of work and out of money. When the TV business was going really great, I had purchased a beautiful dark maroon Stinson 108-3 airplane which we had to sell in order to use the money to live on until I could work again. Later, we were almost out of food and money, and I was still bedfast when our Sunday School class brought us a care package of food. Being unemployed embarrassed me.

"Tomorrow, I'm going to find a job!" I said.

A neighbor who worked at Cobb's Hatchery said they needed another driver. They said it would be an easy job.

"Just drive a semi loaded with 10,000 baby chicks to New York State. They told us the trailer was heated with hot water from the engine. We needed to keep 70 degrees temperature in the trailer so that the chicks wouldn't freeze in the extreme winter cold. The relief driver went to sleep. I noticed the outside temperature was 10 degrees and the trailer temperature was 60. The only way to keep the temperature up was to drive wide open! I drove that way all night, hoping and praying that I wouldn't get caught for speeding.

We arrived at an old Dutch farmer's place in upper state New York. The hatchery told us they had put in 10% overage so that we wouldn't have to count the chicks when we delivered them, but the old Dutch farmers said, "You are going to count every one!"

But he did give us some fellows who helped us count all those chicks. When we got close to the number, he finally said, "That's close enough!"

I was so weak and sick from being out of bed only a couple of days, but I drove most of the way home. My so-called "relief driver" liked to eat big steaks and then go right to sleep!

I vowed all the way home, "I'll never drive another semi!"

When I was well enough, I didn't know exactly where to look for a job. One day, I was at Warren Radio in Elkhart, Indiana, where we bought our TV parts and asked them if they knew anyone that needed an electronic technician. The fellow standing beside me said, "We need one at Sears and Roebuck!"

He took me to Sears, and they hired me right on the spot! I really loved that job. I thought that I had found a job for life. The fellow who got me the job, Frank Hoover and his wife Ramah became life-long friends. Then I got my friend Rich a job at Sears after his uncle with the electrical company passed away.

Rich didn't seem to like the job as much as I did, so later he got a job managing Economy Auto Supply in Goshen, Indiana. After nine years, Sears closed their store in Elkhart, so I went to Montgomery Wards in Goshen where I worked for several years. The service manager for both the Goshen, Indiana, and Niles, Michigan stores asked if I could drive to Niles in the evening, so, it was work, eat fast while driving to Niles, work, drive home, sleep and repeat.

After about a year of this, I was getting worn out. Then my friend Rich got me a job at Economy Auto Supply in Goshen. The store added appliances, TV's, video recorders, cameras, microwave ovens, etc. I retired after 25 years there servicing mostly electronic things.

OTHER HOSPITAL MEMORIES

I went to Goshen Hospital to visit my Uncle Ed who had just had surgery. His room was on the fourth flood. As I stepped into the elevator, a nurse stepped in with a box containing a dozen donuts for the fourth floor nurses' station. The elevator moved up several floors and jerked to a stop. The lights went out, and it was pitch black in there. This was in the day before the emergency light laws were put into place and before cell phones.

After a few minutes in the dark, the nurse began to panic and started to cry. I tried to calm her, but I wasn't feeling too good myself. It was so dark, and we felt like we were going to suffocate.

"Let's have a donut," I suggested. "Maybe that will keep us calm!"

It turns out the hospital was having major construction on it to double the size of the building. A construction worker had accidentally cut the big cable to the elevator. I tried pounding SOS on the wall and someone pounded back. We knew they must be working on the elevator. It took them almost two hours to get the cable spliced and working again. In that length of time, we had devoured all twelve donuts!

When we got out of the elevator, the nurse suddenly said, "I need a restroom! Right away!" She took off running.

Another time when I went to visit Uncle Ed, on the same fourth floor, a nurse came into the room, looked around. She searched in all the corners and wastebaskets. She had a very worried look on her face, and I sensed something was very wrong.

Looking out at the nursing station, I could see some of the nurses were in tears, so I went out there to see if there was anything I could do.

One sobbing nurse said, "We've just received a bomb threat! The caller said the bomb will go off at 3:30! We only have two hours to get everyone out of this hospital."

We used all the wheel chairs, and mustered together all able visitors to help take patients to the elevators and down to the parking lot. We then moved across the street to the lobby of the Goshen College Mennonite Church. We also pushed the bedfast patients across the street, beds, IV's and all! We were quickly out of wheel chairs, but I noticed many of the chairs in the waiting rooms had big casters on them. We put patients in them and pushed them as fast as we could to get them to safety across the street. The hospital had called all local and volunteer fire departments, EMTs and other responders to help. They took all the ICU and heart patients to the Elkhart Hospital.

We had gotten all the patients evacuated—except one. This one was in labor! I stood by her bed. A nurse held her IV, and another nurse stood by waiting for the baby! The baby came, and the three of us were pushing the bed and running as fast as we could to get her across the street. It was exactly 3:20 as we passed through that hospital door! As we exited, the Bomb Squad and the K-9 Bomb-sniffing dogs arrived.

Everyone had safely arrived to the Church lobby across the street.

Many of the older patients in wheel chairs were very upset. They did not understand what was going on. The room was charged with anxiety and fear. Someone decided to get them all milk and cookies. As they settled down with their snacks, we just about collapsed from exhaustion. Later that evening, we were given the "all clear" by the Bomb Squad, but we were so worn out, the local fire department called in volunteers to help get the patients all back to their rooms.

It turned out an exchange student from the college had worked at the hospital and didn't like the way he was treated, so he made the false bomb threat. As for me, it seems like when there's a catastrophe, I somehow happen to be there—especially at the Goshen Hospital, fourth floor!

Then I think of it this way, just "happening to be there" is God's way to "be there" in times of trouble. We never know when we will be called upon, but to those we help, we are God's hands, His arms and His feet to get others to safety and provisions—even in bringing new life into this world.

"ZIB"

The road that led to Alderman Lake was appropriately called Alderman Road, because a prominent family had built the first house on that road. After they died, the road was renamed Hackett Road for the Hackett family who, by the way, developed the Hackett Hotel Chain. They built a very large, beautiful home with two horse barns, servants' quarters, fish ponds. They produced race horses and had vineyards. Their barns were connected by a very large underground tunnel so they could go back and forth without ever going outdoors.

They had a daughter, Elizabeth, known as "ZIB" to all of us. She married a Colonel in WWI, who, even though he was out of the service, wore his uniform, complete with boots and hat. He was a pilot and delivered Luscombe Phantoms from the factory in Trenton, New Jersey. When she was very young, "ZIB" flew a Phantom, powered by a 90 HP Ken Royce radial engine, from the factory to a field on Hackett

Road. She had engine instruments and a compass to navigate by.

The Colonel and "ZIB" ran a flying school on Lakeshore Drive, Chicago, where a golf course is today. A student froze on the controls one day, and they crashed. They survived, but later died of their injuries. "ZIB" closed the flying school and stored the plane in one of the horse barns on Hackett Road. Many years later, she said I could have it. I ran to the barn, only to find some parts and pieces of the plane. Gay and I had built a brick house down the road by this time.

After the Hacketts died, "ZIB" lived there alone. My dad maintained the place until his health declined, and then my uncle maintained it. I then took over the job. By then, she was having a lot of electrical problems. One of the repair jobs took my uncle and me into the tunnel, which was like something from a scary old movie. Deep inside the large cemented tunnel, we found the well and the pump. The switch had gone bad, and it was an easy fix. We noticed large wooden X frames holding about twenty-five small wooden barrels with wooden "bung" valves.

As luck would have it, there was a tin cup right there. We helped ourselves to a small sample from each one.

"This wine gets better and better with each taste," my uncle said, smiling. That was true. By the last sip, it was VERY GOOD!

One day, "ZIB" called and said her lawnmower wouldn't run. I grabbed a can of gas and went over to start it for her. The can contained 145 octane that I used in my "hopped up" gyroplane that I flew in for short air show demos. 145 octane was still available at South Bend Airport, to maintain the DC 7s they had on the premises.

As I poured the gas into the mower, "ZIB" said, "Ahh! AV Gas! I will never forget the smell of AV Gas!"

One New Year's Eve, we had a very bad ice storm. We had decided not to go to the New Year's event at church. However, "ZIB" showed up at our house all "dolled up" with hat, gloves, and a little fur around her neck. She brought us some homemade candy and was going to town to meet her "girlfriends." They were going to a movie and then play bridge. She handed us the candy and said, "Now, don't you kids try to go anywhere! It's really bad out there!"

As the years passed, she called on several occasions to say someone was looking in her window. I would always go, but I never found anything. Then one morning, she called and asked me to come put a back door on the kitchen. I looked at the old door, and it was all splintered and the frame was busted.

"What happened?" I asked.

"He was looking in the kitchen door, so I loaded the double barrel 12-gauge shotgun. I forgot to open the door and pulled both triggers at once."
The "kick" of the shotgun threw her against the back wall, but she never saw another "peeping Tom."

She had asked me to take her up in a Luscombe one more time, but, sadly, she passed away before I could take her. "ZIB" was quite a gal! She passed away in her late nineties—and she is missed!

OUR BRICK HOUSE

Gay and I married in 1952, and we bought a two-car garage, and, with the help of Gay's parents and grandparents, we made a cozy three-room home. Later, we added on and even had a basement with a fireplace. However, we had really wanted a brick house, and I had land at the "home place" on Hackett Road.

Years later, after our sons were born, we found a show house that we liked, and the salesman was from our church. We contracted for them to build one for us. They had just begun construction when the contractor quit. The foreman had to pick up workers wherever he could find them. So, we were off to a rough start. When it came time for the bricks to be laid, the foreman asked us, "Is it ok to have blacks on the job?"

At this time, we had no black people in the Goshen area. They were not allowed to stay overnight in town, and most restaurants would not serve them.

We said, "Sure it's OK with us!"

When they came they said, "The women will lay the bricks, because they are faster than us men, and they lay a really straight pattern. We men mix and keep the mortar going to them. The women do a much better job than we can!"

While they were laying the bricks, we got to know them. They told us that they were both waitresses at a restaurant/bar in Michigan. They wanted us to come there, and they would cook us the "best chicken dinner that you'll ever have!" All our friends told us, "No white people ever go there!"

But Gay's parents enjoyed knowing the group so much, said, "We'll take you there!"

"Bring the kids too!" they said.

One waitress had a nine year old daughter who had grown up in the tavern and loved to play pool. She taught our son Jim how to play pool, and they had a great time. That child could beat any man at pool. She would play one or two rounds with us and then go clean the table. Grant and Jim got along fine with her, and we liked them so well, we ate there several more times.

Our friends at home said, "They might kill you!"

They missed out. We loved them. They eventually showed us their "secret" baseball field behind the tavern, and a team that was just out of this world! They invited National League teams to come and play. No audience. Just two teams playing each other. Their team always won! They did invite us to watch, since they knew Jim was crazy about baseball. They autographed the balls and gave them to the kids when the game was over.

The tavern owner, "Big Jake" told me one day, "Nobody wants to do service work for the blacks in this area. If you would service everyone's appliances and give me all the bills, I will pay you. I did a lot of work in that area, and business was good. As he requested, I took the bills to Big Jake, who not only owned the tavern, but a rooming house and brothel across the street. He would always jokingly say that he didn't have the money to pay me that day, and that I should "go see the ladies across the street!"

I would get so embarrassed! The "ladies" had their own record players that they played in their rooms. Jake had me repair the players, and the women delighted in teasing me. They knew how embarrassed I would get. My face could turn at least fifty shades of red!

Our brick house was our dream house. It had a living room, family kitchen, three bedrooms and one and one half baths. It also had a full basement with pool table, a double finished garage, sliding patio doors to look out over the tree line and wildlife. Since we already owned the land, the house cost us, $11, 940! It wasn't long until the city decided to move the city limits to include all the houses on the north side of Hackett Road. Our taxes were outrageous! They were more than our house payments.

We had to sell the house, and the woman who bought it was known in town as being into politics and speaking her mind. She went to the courthouse steps, and, day after day, she sat there telling everybody about the unfair taxes. About a month later they told her they would give her "free taxes," if she would shut up and stay away from the courthouse. She lived in "the brick house" until she passed away.

Our Brick House on Hackett Road, Goshen, 1967
Lowell, Gay, Grant and Jim

My first flight in my Gyrocopter, "Lady Gay"
I landed in the yard at our new Brick Home!

OUR KIDS AND ALL THOSE OTHER KIDS

Finding time for flying was a real struggle with making a living, raising a family and helping all those other kids who came into our lives. At school, other kids would tell our boys Grant and Jim about their parents' fighting or getting divorced. They were afraid and didn't know what was going to happen to them. Our boys always told them, "You can come and stay with us."

Some stayed a short time, and others stayed for several years. In fact one left, got married, and they came back as a couple to stay a while. There were many sad times and tears, but I am so proud of how they all turned out.

One of the girls thought that cleaning her room meant stuffing everything under the bed and smoothing the bedspread. Another girl thought everything had to be in its place. If it was on the floor, it got thrown out! She cleaned EVERYTHING! One was a very good cook, and we all gained weight when she cooked.

Whenever they got a job, we bought some of them 50-dollar cars and told them they would have to learn to repair them to get to work. They all became good mechanics—even the girls. They could change oil, clean spark plugs, clean carburetors and install brakes. One girl even put a clutch in her car. People joked about how it looked like we had a used car lot! I flew with most of them and taught most of them how to land the plane if it was necessary.

We had a nice wedding for one of the girls, and I worried about them starting life together and making a living. He went to seminary and became a minister. She was a worship leader with a voice like an angel. Needless to say, we are very proud of them. Another girl met a local boy, and we helped with their wedding. They still live in the area and are doing very well.

About 2:30 one morning there was a loud banging on our door. The parents of one of the boys who had been with us for quite a while wanted him back home immediately. It was obvious they were very drunk. They demanded that he leave with them or they would call the police. Since we had no legal rights to him, we had to let the boy go. He was in his pajamas, holding tightly to my leg and crying, "Please don't let them take me!"

They pulled him away from me and stopped down the road to beat him very badly. He ran away from home, and when he was seventeen, he joined the military. We lost track of him until a few years ago, when we were in a restaurant. We heard behind us, "Hi, Mom!" There he sat with his son. He was glad to report they were doing well.

On another occasion, a local couple was getting a divorce. Their five kids were friends of Jim and Grant. The mother came over one hot summer day with the kids and dumped them off, leaving her old International Carryall truck for us to use. I had the day off, so I took all those kids, plus another boy and our two sons to Gay's parents' cottage near Kalamazoo, Michigan. After a day of swimming, all those kids were hungry. I hardly had any money with me, and I had no clue how much it would take to feed all those hungry kids. I went to the country store and bought bread, and laid my money on the counter.

"I want as many hot dogs as this money will buy!"

We cooked them on the outdoor grill, and they ate them as fast as I could cook them!

The old Carryall Truck was so worn out it shimmied badly. I couldn't drive over 45 mph. That was a long trip home. Later the girls went to live with their mother and the boys lived with their dad. The oldest boy came by and stayed with us often.

Many years later, Grant and I were delivering an antique airplane to Maine. We flew into one of the worst lightning and rain storms I had ever seen. We were trying to get over a mountain in the storm because there was an airport on the other side. Grant was flying, and I noticed the trees were very close to us.

"Climb!" I said.

"Dad! We're at full power, and this is as high as the plane will go."

We topped those mountains by about 50 feet. We made the airport and found other people stranded by the storm. We all tried to sleep in a very cold, leaky hangar. The next morning, the guys looked outside.

"How did you get through the mountains? That's the highest mountain, and it's the antenna farm! Some of those antennas are as high as 1000 feet, and they all have guy wires! How in heaven's name did you do that?"

It hit me at that moment. We had flown through all those wires and antennas and never saw a one! Later, we found out that one of those boys who had stayed with us had felt so uneasy about our trip that he had prayed most of the night for us! He was truly one of God's angels.

> *For he will command his angels concerning you to*
> *guard you in all your ways;*
> Psalm 91:11 (NIV)

A BRUSH WITH THE BANDITOS

An old, rusty Volkswagen "bug" sat on the side of County Road 10 just west of Elkhart, Indiana, for several years. I stopped one day to ask about it, and they told me they just wanted to get rid of it. The engine was stuck, and the floor and body were badly rusted. I took it home one Saturday and told the kids they could "play" with it. That is an open invitation for kids aged sixteen and fourteen.

On Sunday, the kids were driving the car around the back yard! Later on, they took the engine and back part off the VW and welded the front frame of a motorcycle to it. After painting it up, they had a really nice three-wheeled motorcycle!

About that time, Gay and I had a chance to go to Arizona with our minister and his wife and another couple from church. My Mom said she would stay with the boys while we were gone. One evening, as she was doing the dishes, she looked out the window to see the well-known motorcycle gang, that had been hanging out in our area since the late 60's, in our front yard. Everyone around was scared of the Banditos, with their loud cycles and rough appearance—black leather vests, chains around their necks. Rumor had it they had even driven their cycles into a supermarket and had taken off with a huge amount of groceries. No one dared to try to stop them! They were the Banditos. Mom was scared to death.

"We're here to take this three-wheeler!" announced the leader of the gang, as he ordered another to grab it. Although there were about twelve of them, Grant grabbed the three-wheeler back from them and a fight started.   Just about that time, Jim let go with our antique 12 gauge shotgun—shooting right over their heads.

According to Jim and Grant, "That old gun shot fire for about ten feet!"

So, after firing a few shots, Jim said to the Banditos gang, "The rest of these shots are gonna be in the seat of your pants!"

At that, the gang scattered and began hopping on their motorcycles and peeling out of our front yard.

Meanwhile, in Phoenix, Gay had gotten sick and fainted. When we got home, our doctor said she needed to have surgery right away. Guess who Gay's roommate was in the hospital? It was the girlfriend of the motorcycle gang leader who was also in for surgery! That evening, Jim and Grant came with me to visit Gay. Shortly after that, the whole gang came in to visit with the girl. Jim and the gang leader talked together like old friends.

Back then, people were kept in the hospital for a longer time. So, after several visits, Jim said, "He's not so bad!" Grant, however, was not so sure about that. He loved his three-wheeled motorcycle and that guy had tried to steal it.

After the story got out, the three-wheeler got to be quite famous in our area. Grant was able to get a good price for it when he decided to sell it. The Banditos finally got run out of the area and went to Ohio. Shortly after that, we heard the leader had been shot and killed in a battle with another gang.

Grant's 3 wheel
Motor Cycle
Bandito's motorcycle
Gang tried to steal it!
Jim saved the day with
12 gauge shot gun

About that 12-gauge shotgun. It had been passed down through several generations of Gay's family. Gay inherited it from her dad. According to her grandfather, it had been used when his family went West. That old gun saved our boys that night from the danger of the Banditos gang, and it saved our lives several other times. Someone tried to rob us in the middle of the night one night, but Jim grabbed that shotgun and shot him in the pants.

He screamed so that I told Jim, "Well, you probably killed him." But he got up and cleared the rail fence in the yard and was last seen going into the corn field. The shells that Jim used were probably 100 years old. Since gun powder gets more potent with age, I think the fire from the gun was as potent as the shells.

Soon after that, the neighbor girls called and said someone had climbed a ladder and was looking into their bedroom window. The parents were not home, and they were frightened; Jim took the gun, snuck out our back door and shot over the guy's head. He fell off the ladder with quite a thud, then took off running through that same cornfield. Wonder how many thugs met up in that corn patch?

THE GREAT GOSHEN ROBBERY

In May of 1970, while working at the service department of Montgomery Ward in Goshen, Indiana, Les Bontrager and I were sent to the warehouse to prep lawn tractors for the summer season. They had been shipped in boxes with the wheels and steering wheels off and no oil or gas in them. Our job was to assemble them and get them ready for the season.

When we arrived, there were several semi's backed up to the loading dock. This was unusual, but we didn't think much about it. As we walked to the warehouse we got a glimpse of a bunch of fellows and suddenly we were hit over the head from behind, pushed to the floor and tied up. Our feet, hands and neck were tied so tightly that, if we tried to move, it tightened the rope on our necks.

An elderly couple had also walked in to pick up merchandise, along with another fellow and his helper. They were also beaten and tied up. The thugs told us they were going to kill us. It turned out the warehouse had just been loaded with appliances, and they were loading it into their semis when we all showed up. They also had many guns and automatic weapons.

It took them quite a long time to load everything into the semis. The guy guarding us kept swearing and telling us he was going to enjoy killing us. After they got the merchandise loaded up, they poured gasoline in a ring around each of us. The gang leader told the fellow guarding us, "Throw your lighter on the gasoline as we leave."

It was rough lying there, thinking we were about to be burnt to a crisp. I am sure we were all praying. Amazingly, we heard sirens screaming toward the warehouse. The robbers jumped into their trucks, and we heard them leave. For some reason, the guy guarding us never threw his lighter on the gasoline.

It turned out the sirens were not coming for us. They were headed for a car wreck that was beyond the warehouse on State Road 4. After the robbers left, one of the fellows who was tied up found a pocket knife they had dropped and managed to cut himself loose. As soon as he was free, he began to scream. Verda Haney, a neighbor lady, heard the screams and rushed over to rub our numb arms and hands. She called the police when she heard us screaming. They soon arrived.

Detective Lester Lung investigated the crime very thoroughly. I told him the fellow guarding us had used the "F" word every few minutes. After a long investigation, some suspects were found, and there was going to be a trial. The Detective said that one suspect used the "F" word all the time, so he was sure he was one of the robbers.

In the meantime, my wife and kids were being followed, and the police told us to carry guns with us and report anything suspicious. On the morning of the trial, I went out to my service truck and saw a guy lurking nearby. I was immediately hit over the head with a pipe from behind. While I was down, he and another kicked me and almost killed me. I can only remember the pointed cowboy boots they kicked me with.

"If any one of your family is called to testify at that trial, you and your family will be killed!"

The suspects got off Scot-free. This was not the way Gay and I had planned to celebrate our eighteenth wedding anniversary-- or the following day, which was my birthday!

The Lord is near to all who call upon Him, to all who call upon Him in truth. He fulfills the desires of those who fear Him. He hears their cry and saves them. Psalm 145: 18, 19

FAMILY VACATIONS

One year, we were given a lake cottage for a week. We only had the 1958 Fiat 500 that I had picked up at the bank that had repossessed it. We loved the car, but it was extremely small. Gay had had more fun piling floral arrangements in it from the shop where she worked and letting them stick out through the sun roof. We never got a picture of that, so Gay drew one!

I had to go to work and took my truck. Gay drove the Bug, and Linda sat in the front with her. For a family vacation, it was entirely too small. Jim and

Grant squeezed into the tiny back seat with a broom and a mop sticking out of that sun roof. We should have gotten a picture of that too.

At the cottage, the boys wanted to fish, but I hadn't brought any fishing gear with me. While I was at work, however, the kids figured out something on their own to fish with. Two older men from the cottage next door came back in their boat. They had fished all morning and caught nothing. They clearly saw that the kids were catching fish, so they walked over and one of them asked, "What are you using?"

Grant replied, "Oh I used a stick and string with an open safety pin for a hook. I stacked the pin with Cheerios. And I made one for my little brother too!"

They were catching fish as fast as they put their hooks into the water! That evening, Mr. Bryant said, "Those kids are the talk of the lake today! Here we are with expensive spinning rods and bait that we bought and never got a bite. Here are these two little kids getting fish with Cheerios and safety pins!"

A few years later, the boss gave me a week off, but Gay and I said we didn't have money to go anywhere. The boss and I were discussing it when a friend overheard us.

"You're welcome to use our hunting cabin on Big Manistee Lake in Upper Michigan, 35 miles north of the Mackinaw Bridge at Engadine. My boys and I use it only for hunting, but you can use it anytime in the summer for fishing."

We had an old VW bus with 150 thousand miles on it, but we thought it would make the trip and be economical. We took an iron skillet, tomatoes, bread, cereal, tater tots, and milk in an ice chest along with what little money we had. We didn't realize there was a five-dollar fee to cross the bridge! But we paid and made it to the cabin. It was seven miles to the nearest house and had bunks upstairs and down. There was a wood-burning cook stove and a gas lantern for light. For water, we had to prime the well.

We rented a boat at Engadine and went fishing. At first we didn't have any luck catching fish, and the boys were getting hungry. I saw a sandy cove and decided to go to shore there.

"I'll start a campfire and we can have tater tots and bread sandwiches," I told them.

The boys waded out and fished while I got the fire going, and suddenly, they began to catch a lot of perch. We had a real good lunch and went back out on the lake to fish some more. Later that day, we got some nice bass and called it a day. We went back to the cabin to clean fish. It was getting dark, so we hung the lantern and started cleaning fish on the board that was fastened between two trees.

Every time we threw fish heads into the woods we would hear a big SLURP. The bears caught the heads before they even touched the ground. We finished cleaning and got ready for bed. We heard noises outside the walls. It turns out the bears were rubbing their backs on the corner of the log cabin. In the morning the kids wanted to feed the bears, so they used their bowls and put cereal and milk in them. The bears ate the cereal and the plastic cereal bowls.

The next morning, Gay went to the "outhouse," and when she opened the door, she screamed. She saw a huge bear napping in the sun in the middle of the path that led to the house. He wouldn't wake up. Gay sat patiently in the outhouse as the boys and I made noise. The bear finally got up and sauntered into the woods.

We got ready to go home and paid the boat rental. That left us with $5.50 and a few snacks to get us home. The bridge, of course, took $5 of that money, so we had fifty cents to get home on. This was before credit cards. We got to Middlebury and ran out of gas. The attendant looked at me rather funny when I asked for 50 cents worth of gas. The old VW made it into our driveway before it ran out of gas. Talk about Someone watching out for us, He did that trip.

By the time we took another vacation, we were driving a really old, but nice, Chevy Impala, along with a trailer to take the Gyro Copter to Rockford, Illinois.

It was going to be the last EAA Fly In to be held there. I wanted to fly in, so we pulled onto a side road a few miles from Rockford. I unloaded the copter and flew in, while Gay and the boys drove the car and trailer into the camp grounds. We had our nice four-foot wall tent and two pup tents. Gay and I were going to use the big tent, but the boys and their friend Greg had already set up the big tent.

By this time, the boys were old enough to be into guitars and music. Grant had built an amplifier for the electric guitars. He rigged the amplifier and one light bulb to work off the car battery. So, the boys, plus kids they met at Rockford took over the big tent. Guess where Gay and I wound up? The pup tent was cozy, and my bare feet stuck out. The next morning, we saw there was ice on the tent.

The kids played music into the wee hours. The next night after supper, they were missing. We looked all over and couldn't find them. We also found that two of Woody Pusher Designer Harry Wood's sons were also missing. We had just about everyone at the fly in looking for those kids. About midnight, they came walking in.

"WHERE have you been?"

"Why, we've just been down at the Woody Pusher talking about airplanes! We lost all track of time."

Despite the scare, we had a great time at the fly-in. However, when we got ready to leave, we found the car battery was dead from running the guitar amp all week. We have great memories of that last fly-in at Rockford!

TEEN AGE BOYS AND THEIR JOBS

When our son Grant was in high school, he got a job at the bakery in Goshen, where he made pies and donuts and other baked delights. These had to be delivered to restaurants and coffee shops very early in the morning. He had a key to the shop and started work at 4:30 each morning so he could get them delivered. Gay had to drive him to work for a while, since he didn't have his drivers license yet. She loved driving the VW Powered fiber glass dune buggy that Grant had built. It had a top that had zip-in windows and very wide, slick tires.

The police stopped them in the alley and asked what a woman in her PJ's and a teen age boy were doing at that time of the morning in a dune buggy. Grant gave the policeman the phone number of the bakery's owner and everything got straightened out. On a later morning, after Grant had his motorcycle license he rode his motorcycle to work and again had to explain to the police why he was out in the wee hours going to work at the bakery.

At Easter time, the bakery had a big display in the front window with Easter eggs and a baby bunny rabbit. When Easter was over, Grant brought the rabbit home for a pet. "George" grew to be a very large rabbit—white with black spots. He was house broken, and often slept with the kids.

One day, when we had been gone, we came home to find that "George" had chewed the living room drapes off as high as he could reach. He also chewed a light cord off. Gay put him outside to live. The boys worried about him until the next spring, when the forty-acre field behind the house was filled with brown bunnies that had lots of black and white spots. We think "George" found a mate and had his own family!

Our son Jim soon wanted to earn money for a car, so he got a job at the Holiday Inn as a bus boy. It was the "in" place to eat, especially after church on Sunday. He wore a white shirt and black pants. We told him often how handsome he looked.

One evening after they closed, the employees decided to go for a swim in the Inn's pool. We began to worry when Jim didn't get home at the usual time. It wasn't long till we heard his motorcycle in the driveway. He told us the employees were going swimming in the hotel pool and asked if he wouldn't like to join them. Well, of course he did!

I WANNA BE A FLY BOY

We had an old "Michigan basement" in our home place when I was a kid. Over in a dark corner of that basement I built a bench and some shelves and wired one light bulb over the bench. I spent many hours there drawing model airplanes and building balsa wood, rubber band-powered models.

I saved my paper route money until I could buy a gas engine, which was an Olsen-Rice 23. It had a regular coil spark ignition and a carburetor. These engines were usually hard to start, but from them I learned a lot about engines that I would use later in life. I made free flight airplanes, trimmed to fly in a circle, and a timer to cut off the fuel so they wouldn't fly too far.

I was afraid of losing the plane, so I started building U-controlled models with 35-foot lines flying in a circle. I made a very nice circle track to take off and land on. This almost required two people—one to start and hold the model, and one to be in the center of the circle to fly the airplane. I crashed a lot trying to learn how to fly U-controls.

My dad worked very hard at C. G. Conn's in Elkhart, Indiana, and then drove home to work on the farm till dark. But if I had the model already to go when he got home, he would start and launch the plane for me. Even though there was always plenty of work to do, Dad always took time for me.

I soon got a radio-controlled model that still had the old vacuum tubes and the big batteries. The last time that I flew it, the batteries went dead, and I lost control and the plane. I jumped on my bike and rode as fast as I could, but after several miles, it flew off in the distance. I never found it, so I lost my new motor and also interest in model flying until our sons began flying RC models at our home air strip. Today, many RC fliers come to our strip to fly their models.

As with most of us in aviation, model airplane building and flying led to the love and career flying "real airplanes." Once an airplane junkie, always an airplane junkie. It seems like such a short time ago I was riding my bike to the airport, hoping to wash a plane for a ride in it. I think of how the pilots trusted this young kid with their airplanes. Back then, it was all about the airplanes, but now I look back and realize it was really the people that I met who formed my life as a pilot.

The early pilots, instructors and airport managers trusted me to clean and fly and put their airplanes away. They even trusted me to fly with students and show them how to do crosswind landings. They had to know I didn't have a pilot's license yet, but they had no clue. They just figured I did. Well, they never asked me, so I never told them any differently.

Many years later, I think of how the Northern Indiana Air Museum trusted me with their priceless aircraft. They trusted me to fly them at air shows all over the Midwest. I have taken many people on their first "War Bird" rides. Now, in my mid-eighties, I realize how many of these people trusted me and helped form me into the person I am today!

AIRPLANE JUNKIE

I think back to the first flights in all those different airplanes that had so many different engines. Back in those days, we never got checked out in an airplane. We just jumped in and checked ourselves out. As WWII ended, there were surplus airplanes all over the place. Sadly, most of them were worn out.

The PT-19's and PT-26's were the first ones to be surplused out. The Ranger Engine was a big inverted six-cylinder engine and had very different characteristics than the round engines. I had to learn those characteristics. Since it was inverted and worn out, oil ran down on the spark plugs and would "foul" them out. I learned that part of my pre-flight preparation was to clean the plugs and clean all the fuel and oil screens and then do a very thorough pre-flight inspection. As a young man, I was taking off in a plane that I had never flown. I figured I had about 300 miles to learn the engines and how to fly it before I had to land it. I eventually got to pick up many PT-19's.

One hot day, I was flying a PT-19 back, and it started to miss badly. I saw a nice farm pasture, so I landed there. The farm lady asked if there was anything she could do to help. I asked her if she had any ice. She fetched me a pan full and looked at me kind of funny.

"You going to fix it with ice?"

"Yes, Ma'am!" I said as I packed the mags in ice.

The engine started right up and ran fine for the rest of the trip.

Several years later, I was flying a PT-26 across Illinois, and it started to miss--same Ranger Engine, same characteristics. I thought it was going to quit, so I looked for a good landing spot. Lo, and behold! There was the same farm I had landed on in the PT-19! I put the plane on the ground and shut it off. Almost immediately I heard a familiar voice.

"You need more ice?" It was the same lady!

"Yes, Ma'am!" I said, and we both had a good laugh.

I packed the mags. They cooled down, and soon I was headed home!

Later, I went to pick up my first Stearman. I had never even been close to one before. I climbed into the cockpit and looked down. It seemed so big and so high up off the ground. It had a side crank starter, so I had to get a helper to do the cranking to start the Continental 220 Engine. This engine needs the oil temperature to be 40 degrees Centigrade before you can increase the RPM. There is nothing like sitting in that cockpit listening to that engine warm up!

I had to learn about round engines and about oil collecting in the lower cylinders. I grew to enjoy the round engines. Each one has its own personality and if you listen to them, they will tell you something is wrong before it breaks! I really love round engines and the bigger, the better! The Pratt and Whitney 985's were kind of a gold standard, and P & W 1340's and 2800's were simply works of art!

AERONCA CHAMP

I have so many fond memories of the Aeronca 7FC Tri Traveler, it's hard to count them. I was at the Goshen Airport, and, as usual, no one else was around. There sat a brand new Aeronca 7FC that had just been flown in by a factory delivery pilot. The Goshen College Aero Club had ordered it to be their Club airplane. The Tri Traveler was the first tri-gear aircraft made by Aeronca. This one, N9859B, was manufactured in 1958. I can still smell the fragrance of the dope paint and 80 octane gas, also known as "the old red gas".

"Hey! You want to take it around the field?" I heard a voice getting closer to me. I jumped. I was just 25 years old, and the fellow didn't even know me.

"You ever flown an Aeronca Champ?"

"Yes!" I answered almost shouting.

"Well, this one's the same thing, only easier!"

He never asked me if I had a license! I just jumped in and flew it around. I fell in love with that plane immediately. Years later, the Goshen College Aero Club disbanded, and the plane was sold to an old fellow from Wakarusa, Indiana. I kept trying to buy it from him, and finally, as he got older, he said he would sell it to me at a low price, IF I would take him for a ride in it whenever he wanted to go flying. He always wanted to fly it to Wakarusa and circle his house, and then fly back to the Goshen Airport. I did that many times.

Our two boys also fell in love with the Aeronca.

"Dad, you can't sell that plane until we get married and move away!" So I didn't.

I keep a large colored photo of it on top of the TV—right where I can look at it anytime. Some airplanes can just become part of the family. I had overhauled it and recovered it at 2500 hours. I overhauled it again at 4000 hours. I don't know how many hours are on it today. It's had many owners since.

Our Aeronca 7FC

COUSIN SHIRLEY

My cousin Shirley came to live with us when she was a little girl. She and I did a lot of things together, and I was always telling her about airplanes and cars. She loved to help working on cars. My first car was a Model A Ford. After we got it running, I was able to get a '34 Plymouth. It didn't run, and the brakes didn't work. Shirley and I towed it home, but, hey, it was "almost free!"

It needed a lot of TLC, so Shirley and I worked on it all the time. The biggest problem was the brakes. The '34 Plymouth was the first to use hydraulic brakes, and the material that they used would not hold up well with the hydraulic fluid. Getting the right material and learning how hydraulics worked would be saving lives later in life.

Shirley graduated from high school, and since she had heard so much from me about airplanes, she decided to go to school to be a stewardess. After graduating from Stewardess School, she got a job with Lake Central Airlines out of South Bend, Indiana. She really loved her job. From time to time, I would pick her up, because I loved the DC-3s. Sometimes my sister Caroline and her husband Johnny also picked her up and she would stay with us until her next flight.

After several years, I noticed that the DC-3's one engine would be nice and clean, like brand new, but the other one would be oily with streaks of oil on the wing. I asked Shirley about it.

"Lake Central is having a few financial problems, so we keep one good engine, and one run-out engine on the other side. We often have to clean the spark plugs on the run-out engine at Denver before we return to South Bend."

She loved the job, but back then you couldn't be a stewardess if you were married. She wanted to get married, so she retired. On one of her last flights to Denver — a night flight with bad storms all the way — the landing gear wouldn't come down on arrival at Denver. She overheard the pilot and co-pilot discussing circling until they were low on fuel and hope the storm would pass before they would have to "belly it in."

Shirley knew the DC-3 well, and knew there was a panel in the cabin that they could remove to access the hydraulic tank. She suggested to the pilot that she would brew up some thick coffee to pour in for hydraulic fluid.

"Don't bother us, we have an emergency!" the pilot snapped. The continued flying.

Later the Co-pilot thought it might be a good idea, and that they should at least try it. He didn't like the idea of "bellying the plane in" during a storm either. They agreed, and Shirley poured the coffee in as they tried lowering the landing gear. It went down perfectly!

At her retirement party, they gave Shirley a plaque and a speech about her saving the plane and the passengers. She later told me that if we hadn't worked on that old car with all those hydraulic issues, she wouldn't have understood enough about the systems to make it work!

Shirley married Dave Slaybaugh, who was making a career of the military. She followed him to California and several countries. On his third tour of Viet Nam, Dave was to lead a patrol at night. They got into a fire fight and were pinned down on a hill. His tour would have been up the next day, but since they were under fire, they had one chopper to relieve them. The men wanted him to go since his tour was up, but he would not leave his men.

The fight lasted almost a week until some choppers came in and picked the soldiers up. The chopper that Dave was in crashed, and his back was broken. He had a long recovery and was sent back to Ft. Lee, Virginia. Now, as Colonel C. David Slaybaugh, he arranged to take me for a tour of the base. Every place we went, he was saluted and so was I. I was embarrassed that the soldiers saluted the car as we drove by. Dave laughed his famous laugh.

"Oh! They think you are a VIP."

OTHER SPECIAL AIRPLANES

One dealer liked Stinson Airplanes and said he noticed when I took rides in it they seemed to sell quicker.

"Why don't you take one of the Stinsons and fly it as it was yours until it sells, and then I'll get you another one!" That sounded like a good deal to me!

I had two Stinson 108-2 Voyagers and then later two Stinson 180-3 Station Wagons. The last one was dark maroon with a polished wood interior. I bought that one and have many fond memories of it.

When our son Grant was about four years old, he would stand between my legs and fly the airplane. On a trip to Illinois, he flew the whole trip. Jim was only two, but very anxious to go for an airplane trip. He went to sleep as we were taking off and climbing out. He didn't wake up until we got out of the plane at Milford, Illinois. He cried inconsolably because he had missed the flight!

When I was a young kid, I knew a lady pilot who gave me a ride in a 40 hp Taylorcraft. It was solid black with red trim. That ride thrilled me! Later, she bought a Piper Tri Pacer. It happened that year that Goshen had a big flood. Goshen was like a lake as far as the eye could see! She wanted so badly to see the flood from the air, but the Tri Pacer was down for maintenance. I let her go up in my Stinson 108-3. She flew all over the area to look at the flooded areas and really fell in love with the plane. We traded airplanes a lot from then on. For her 95th birthday, a bunch of us pilots organized a "fly out" to dinner for her. She was thrilled beyond imagination.

"This is a great celebration, but plan a really big one for my 100th birthday "fly out".

At 96.5 years, she flew from Indiana to Arizona to visit her brother—ALONE! Her children were very upset that she had done this without telling them.

"You didn't think that I would drive that far, did you?" she scoffed. "That would be dangerous!"

A year later, at 97.5 years of age, a car ran into her, resulting in a very bad crash. She died from complications of the accident. She proved that the only thing that is scary about flying is driving to the airport.

She had two sons, and I flew with them also. Her oldest son and very pregnant wife accompanied Gay and me in the Stinson to a big fly in in Ohio. On the run up, as we got ready to leave, one magneto failed.

We sat there deciding what to do, when I said, "That's why we have two magnetos!" I took off, and we flew home just fine!

Later, when I thought about that decision, I said to myself, "I'll NEVER do that again."

But I did do it again many years later. We were flying a Waco YMF-5 to Ft. Wayne, Indiana, Smith Field, where we took rides all day long. It was a very hot day, and when we got ready to fly home, one ignition system failed. The Waco uses one magneto and one distributor ignition system. The coil for the ignition system had overheated and burned up.

The anxious pilot/owner asked, "How are we going to get home?"

I answered, "Oh. We've got one good magneto, we'll be fine!"

The owner happened to be an airline captain—they just do not fly if the plane has issues! I finally convinced him that we would be just fine. He took off and climbed to over 10,000 feet. He stayed at 10,000 feet all the way home, until we were over our home strip. We landed fine, and after searching, we found a new coil for the old Jacobs engine. The owner called several parts places and found one coil still in the original box in Oklahoma. When he received it, I installed it, and it's still running fine today. I know that God watches over us, even when we do dumb things!

The LORD watches over you—
the LORD is your shade at your right hand;
the sun will not harm you by day,
nor the moon by night.
The LORD will keep you from all harm—
he will watch over your life;
the LORD will watch over your coming and going
both now and forevermore.
Psalms 121:5-8

READ THE FINE PRINT

I guess I shouldn't leave you guessing how I became part owner of a B-29 and a PT Boat. When World War II ended, all that military stuff went on a Government Bidders List. The list came out once a month with everything from office equipment to airplanes, jeeps, tanks and other miscellanea.

Three of us guys got together once a month when the list came out, hoping to get an L-4 Airplane or an L-19. But we never had that kind of luck. After a few months, we saw that our bids were not enough. I guess we got a little bit "Slap happy," so, as a joke, we bid $5.00 on a lot of items.

One day, we received an OFFICIAL LETTER stating that no one else had bid on the B-29 or the PT Boat. We were "awarded" both of them. The letter also stated that our bids were accepted, and we would owe storage fees until they were removed from government property. We would also be responsible for any charges, such as loading and moving!

The B-29 was located at Davis-Monthan Air Salvage in Arizona, and the PT Boat was located at Norfolk Naval Yard in Virginia! Most of us guys had hardly been out of Indiana! I didn't get to go to Tucson, AZ, but the other two went. They had to pay $1000 to get the airplane ready to fly just a few miles to Tucson International. They HAD to remove it from the salvage yard. Then they had to pay a pilot and co-pilot $1000 to fly the plane to Tucson International, where they also had to pay another $1000 for fuel. They were scared to death, because, back then, none of us had that kind of money to even spend on "needed stuff." We always thought an extra $50 in the pocket was a fortune!

Our folks were about ready to disown us when we wanted to borrow money. One fellow's parents were so sure that the government would come after them to pay the bills. One day, my two friends were eating in a restaurant. The word had gotten out about those two crazy kids that ended up with a B-29. It was also the first year that the orange groves expected an early frost.

One of the grove owners came up to them and said, "Hey, kids! I'll give you $1000 for each engine and the mounts. I can use them to blow air over the orange groves to keep them from freezing."

The airport was also charging by the pound for the B-29 to sit on the tarmac. A lady that owned some ground next to the airport got an idea. She wanted to drag the plane over to her property and start a hot dog stand in it! She had a ladder made that went to the front of the fuselage, with a kitchen down one side of the interior. You could get a hot dog, all the fixin's, and a drink and exit the back stairs to the tables and chairs located under the wing. She   paid the remainder of the bill—so we broke even!

God took care of us, by turning our mess into a miracle! One word to the wise, however, if you get on the bidders list, be sure you read the fine print!

And we know that in all things
God works for the good of those who love him,
who have been called according to his purpose.
Romans 8:28

B-29 like the one we got for "only five dollars!"

PT BOAT OWNERS—FOR A WHILE

World War II PT boats were originally built with three Cadillac 8-cylinder gas engines. By the end of the war, they were putting two Cummins 500 HP diesel engines in them to get more power and more range out of them. The boat that our $5.00 bid won was one of the later ones with the diesels. I got to go to Norfolk with my buddies to collect our treasure.

Upon arriving, we were told that a harbor pilot would have to drive it a certain distance off shore before we could drive it. The cost for the harbor pilot and a Coast Guard boat to take him back to the dock would be $100. Besides, they had also just put $400 worth of fuel in it.

Les Koher, one of my buddies, was into scuba diving and sail boats, so the harbor pilot OK'd Les to drive the boat. We had a lot of fun driving up the East Coast to the St. Lawrence Seaway. I lost track of all the negotiations and money it took us to get back to Lake Michigan, but every lock cost $100 to pass through. It was a very long trip!

Les's uncle had purchased a lot on the beach at New Buffalo, Michigan, to build a cottage. He had not been able to get a permit, however, because of a Beach Preservation Group, but he could park a boat there. We beached the boat there, with still no idea how we were going to pay for this "great deal" we had gotten.

One day, while working in New Paris, Indiana, was eating in the restaurant with Fred Slabaugh, who was putting in the new overhead road in town. His big earth mover had just blown the engine, which happened to be a Cummins diesel. He asked me about our boat engines. It turned out they were the exact same engines that were on the boat!

Fred gave us $5000 for the two engines and took them out of the boat. With the boat beached on his property, he was able to make a fine cottage out of it. It had a stainless steel kitchen, and could sleep six people, with three bunks on each side. So the PT Boat story had a very happy ending—for Les and me and for Uncle Fred—once again proving Romans 8:28 to be absolutely true!

On a side note, recently, at our EAA Chapter 132 Christmas Party, a fellow who knew about the PT Boat story came up to me and said, "What a coincidence!

After World War II, my friend who was a scuba diver got a PT boat on the government bidders list, and paid $2000 for it."

It turns out that they picked it up at Norfolk, Virginia, at the same dock we got ours from. As we talked, we realized we must have been there around the same time. Their boat was an early model which had three V-8 Cadillac engines in it. They also had to pay for a lot of gasoline with those three engines. They also had to pay the Coast Guard Pilot to take it out of the dock area and used the same route as we had to get up to the St. Lawrence Seaway at the cost of $100 per driver for each of the locks. They also had the same problems navigating the route to Lake Michigan. They were also able to use their boat to take tourists for scenic rides.

We had a grand time talking and realizing we had shared the same experience all those years ago.

This is JFK's PT 109. Ours looked just like it, but we
only paid $5 for it!

EXCITEMENT IN THE AIR

After most of the surplus planes ran out, I had stopped picking up planes for dealers. Then and old friend called and asked me to pick up his plane and fly it back to Goshen. He had flown it to a good FBO Service center to have a condition inspection but had developed some serious health issues and could not pick up the plane. I agreed to do it for him.

It had been a year since my friend had flown the plane to the FBO, and it would need another condition inspection before it could be flown. Everything seemed to be okay, except the right aileron seemed to have too much play in its push rod and bell crank. This troubled me, so I talked it over with the A/E who said he knew that, but it had been flown like that for years.

The airplane was a bi-plane built with a Pitts fuselage and Smith mini plane wings. I took off and climbed out, leveled off, and the airspeed passed through 100 MPH. It was then that the right aileron began to flutter. It shook so hard that the right wings looked like they were two feet thick. I was convinced those wings were going to come off any minute.

127

I snapped the throttle off and pulled the nose up to slow flight. Suddenly the flutter stopped, and it had jerked the control stick right out of my hand. I carefully tried the control stick, and the right aileron didn't even move. I tried the left stick, and the aileron moved. I very carefully kept the plane in slow flight, straight ahead, no turns. I then very slowly landed it at the Goshen Airport, straight ahead, no turns. It was a good landing.

In checking the plane, I found that when the right aileron fluttered so hard, the right control bell crank had pulled its bolts right through the spar. God had been watching over me.

The owner sold the plane to a local fellow, who did a very careful job of repairing the right wing. He flew down and landed on our strip to tell me how nice it flew. Later on, he sold it to another friend of ours from Michigan. This friend flew with a very small Poodle dog. The dog had his own parachute, and they tell me they even tried it once. He flew down to our place many times, and every time he would do spins before he landed. That Poodle loved the spins.

He developed heart trouble and had to have a heart transplant. Sadly, he had to sell the plane. Another pilot in Michigan bought it and took it home very late one evening. It was getting dark, and the pilot flew through electric wires at a little private airfield. The plane had hit electric wires, but there was almost no damage, so he quickly put the plane in the hangar and locked the door. The whole surrounding area was without power. The lineman asked him if he saw a plane hit the wires.

"No. I just got here," he answered.

He left his hangar locked for a few months until everyone had forgotten the episode.

It is interesting to note that the plane was built by a fellow named Bill Williams, and the next four owners were all named Bill. As far as I know, the last Bill still owns the plane!

FLYING WITH KEITH

My cousin Keith and I enjoyed a lot of flying together. Keith was a coach and teacher in Crawfordsville, Indiana, and, early on, Keith would fly his 1939 Aeronca Chief up to Goshen. Later, he sold it and, together, he and I bought a 1946 Aeronca Champ. We took turns having the plane for a month. I would fly it to Crawfordsville to pick him up, and he would fly me home and take the plane for a month. After the month, he would fly to Goshen and pick me up, so I could take the plane home for "my" month.

These back and forth trips gave me some interesting experiences. One time, when I was flying the Champ to Keith's, I ran into a bad late-afternoon storm. It had a lot of lightning in it, so I had to fly around it. In doing so, I got lost, and by the time I found out where I was, I was very low on fuel. I had to find the nearest field with fuel to get down. I saw an old biplane sitting in a field and chose it. The field looked very short, but I landed, and as I taxied up to the gas pump, I ran out of gas.

It turned out that field really was an airport, but a very small one in Mulberry, Indiana, run by "Pop" Stair. He had received his Pilot's License from the Wright Brothers themselves, and he was still barnstorming with an old Waco 9. I told him I needed gas.

"I know! I saw that you were out of gas when you rolled to a stop," he said.

"I was sure worried about landing in such a short field!" I said.

After gassing up, he said, "Get in, and I'll show you how to take off from a real short field!"

"Oh! You don't want both of us in the plane on this short field," I protested.

"That's what I'm going to show you! We're gonna taxi down to the far end, and we'll be heading toward the fence at almost 40 MPH. Then we're gonna hit full left rudder and full left brake, make a 180 degree turn coming to full power at just the right time, and we'll be off in no time!"

He took off and showed me how it worked, and then made me do it. I realized that by learning this maneuver, it got me out of some very tight places when I was picking up surplus planes through the years.

Many years later, I was flying down that way and looked down at that same little airport. By this time, "Pop" Stair was in his late 90's, and he still remembered the day I landed back then. I remembered how good his coffee was. I had been so nervous that day, and the coffee really helped! There on the pot belly wood stove sat that coffee pot! I pointed to it, smiling.

"Well, it's the same coffee as when you were here before. I never change it! I just add to it!"

I didn't believe him, but it sure tasted good!

Keith and I flew the Champ back and forth many times, but we soon decided we wanted something a little faster. We settled on a surplus PT-22 with a Kenner R56 radial engine. We both loved flying it, but the old Kenner engine was kind of like an old tractor engine. You had to know how to treat it and how to "talk" to it to keep it running.

The Kenner uses carb heat on only one cylinder. Carb heat alone is not enough to clear the ice. You have to make it backfire to blow the ice out. One day after school, Keith took a student for a ride in the PT-22, it quit because of carb ice. He got the ice cleared, but it came back a second time. The engine quit, so he tried to make the airport. The plane stalled, however, and they crashed. The plane was totaled, but, thank the Lord, Keith and his passenger had only minor injuries to their foreheads from the instrument panel.

One time in Crawfordsville, I needed a ride back home. A fellow at the airport had heard us talking and asked me if I would fly his plane to Goshen. He had a brand new Piper PA-14 Family Cruiser. He needed to go to Goshen, but he had been partying and drinking a LOT! Would I fly him to Goshen?

I had never seen a PA-14 before, but I told him, "Sure, I'll fly you to Goshen."

He went to sleep on takeoff and slept all the way to Goshen. That plane flew so nice! Being brand new, I really enjoyed it! I tied it down at Goshen Airport, and tried to wake him up, but he just wanted to sleep. So, I let him sleep and went home. I never saw the man again. I guess he made it wherever he was going.

Our family Dentist was a great friend and avid fisherman. He had heard about some great fishing on a river up in Michigan. He said he sure would love to go there and check it out.

"I'll fly you up there in my Luscombe," I said.

We flew up to Big Rapids, Michigan, Airport, and, just a short walk across the highway was the Big Rapids River.

We spent quite a while walking up and down the river bank and talked with a couple of fishermen. They confirmed that it was the greatest fishing around!

The little airport was a nice one with a new black top runway and a nice office. However, it was unattended. The gas pumps were turned on, and a cigar box with money in it had a sign on it saying, "Make your own change!"

My dentist friend said he couldn't believe that they could trust people for fuel and payment! I told him at that time it was common for airports to do this. I knew of airports where you pumped your own fuel and made your own changes.

Later, on another trip to that airport, I mentioned to one of the fellows that my friend couldn't believe they left the money in the cigar box.

To that, the fellow said, "Ya know? We've never had fuel stolen or any money taken, and some people even leave a little extra!"

Wow! Don't you wish we could do that today?

PASSION DOESN'T ALWAYS MAKE GOOD SENSE

My passion for flying over the years took many forms. While still in high school, I realized that flying was costing me too much for me to have an airplane. I later decided I would build a gyrocopter, since I could build it in the garage and keep it at home. I built the gyrocopter and read Benson's book on how to fly them. I took it to the Goshen Airport where I took off in it and, since I flew it successfully, I flew it home and landed in our backyard. A neighbor lady called the sheriff, so I never did that again.

Although I had flown the first flight, I had really not learned to fly a gyrocopter! On the second flight, I had it porpoising. (PTO's) I came close to being killed. A helicopter and gyrocopter instructor had witnessed this. We found paint marks under the rotor where the prop tip had touched the bottom of the rotor. I was that close to cutting the rotor and crashing. The instructor gave me a long talk and chewed me out. I then spent a lot of time researching porpoising in gyroplanes. I wrote many articles the PRA (Popular Rotocraft Association) Magazine, hoping to save someone from getting into trouble. We had a great group of people and formed PRA Chapter 34. We had monthly fly-ins at Knox, Indiana, and Coldwater, Michigan. We were a close-knit group, enjoying picnics, dinners and even dancing.

At one of our fly-ins we guys flew the copters to a park in Winamac, Indiana. The women brought the cars, trailers and food. Trailers were a necessity, because, most of the time the old Mac drone engines would not start when hot. We enjoyed a very good dinner and fellowship, but noticed a storm brewing. Everybody loaded their copters onto their trailers. Mine was the only one that would start, so I decided to fly back to Knox. The storm caught up with me just as I approached Knox. I was flying with my camera around my neck, so I took a picture of the storm. It became my favorite picture. One the left side of the picture, it is pouring down rain, but on the right side it was bright and sunny. A minute later, I got drenched.

Several years later at a fly-in at Knox, I was doing a 12-15 minute show that I had developed with my gyroplane. I had replaced the cylinders on the old Mac with some from a high altitude drone that had more compression and power. I had to use 145 octane fuel, which could still be purchased at the South Bend,

Indiana, Airport. They needed it for the DC-7 airliners. I started my routine with an agreement that, if an airplane came into the pattern, that I would "give way" to it. A Piper Cherokee entered the pattern, so I climbed very high over the airport. I cut the throttle and spiraled down. As I approached final, I was dropping more than expected, so I gave it full throttle, producing a big explosion. I could see the terrified face of a lady in a car on Highway 35. I landed just on the end of the runway, and people told me I had ten feet of fire following me across the highway. The old Mac had just blown up.

One beautiful day a lot of gyrocopters were flying in and out of Coldwater, Michigan. Later in the afternoon I took off and turned right over US Highway 12. I blew a cylinder on the rebuilt Mac, so I turned back across the drive-in theater. I was about halfway up the screen and landed on the last ten feet of runway. Another member was flying his Mac and approaching at the other end of the runway, putting his approach over a lake. He blew a cylinder over the lake and went in about ten feet from shore. The guys all jumped in and pulled him and his copter out. He and the copter were both okay.

On another Knox Fly-in, I was flying home and stopped in Warsaw, Indiana at the airport for gas. The engine seemed very hot when I started to leave. It was a hot day, so I didn't think any more about it. As I flew over Milford Lake, the beach was full of swimmers. Lots of pretty girls in swimsuits were waving at me! So, I circled several times and was leaving the lake, flying over the big woods, and BANG! The engine stopped. I made it past the last tree and landed almost straight down, bending the axle a little, but not too badly. The crank shaft had broken in the center main bearing, from actually melting in the center. It was exciting, but that is the way it was with those Mac Drone engines!

I finally had enough of blowing out cylinders on the old Mac drone engines, so I built a new copter with an aircraft engine and better blades. It was a heavier machine and was soon ready for its test flight. I called Igor Benson about it.

"It won't work!" he protested. "I've already tried that! The power and weight ratio is just not good enough."

A local mechanic that built engines for Reno Air racers told me, "Bring me your engine! We'll fix it!"

I picked up the engine and put it on my copter. The mechanic said to turn the RPM up and suggested the kind of prop I should use. It worked so well, and the tests went so well that I took it to Oshkosh/EAA AirVenture Fly-In and won the Man and Machine Award! Everybody wanted one, so I sold plans.

As they built them, they told me they didn't have enough power to fly out of ground effect. So I went to my mechanic and asked him what he had changed on my engine.

He just smiled and said, "A race mechanic never tells his secrets!"

I had to tear my engine down to find out what he had done, and then we were able to get the other copters flying.

SPEAKING OF ENGINES

When people ask me how many engine failures I've had over the years, I always tell them, "Engines weren't as reliable back then as they are today."

My first "engine out" happened when I borrowed a worn out Aeronca Champ to run some parts to Hastings, Michigan. This was before I had a pilot's license, but it was a lot more fun to fly than to drive. When I took off from Hastings and was climbing out, the engine just stopped!

I was over the woods with big trees everywhere. I had no place to go, but in my head I could hear, "Land straight ahead; do not turn around!"

However, with no place to go, I made a hard turn around, pushed the nose down to keep from stalling, and took a few branches out of a tree. I made a safe landing with no damage to the airplane! It turned out that a rotor in a magneto had come apart in such a way that it shorted out both mags. The mechanic said he had a pair of "kinda worn out" old mags, but they were better than the ones I had. Since I only had $5.00, he said he would trade my mags for his.

My first "engine out" was quite exciting, but, little did I know, this was to be the first of many.

When I started to pick up surplus aircraft, most of them had been worn out by the military. The PT's had a lot of trouble with overheating mags. They would begin misfiring and would soon quit. I had a lot of off-field landings to fix the mags.

The inverted engines, like Ranger engines, would collect oil in the cylinders and you had to be very careful to turn them slowly to get all of the oil out of the cylinders. If you got in a hurry and didn't get all of the oil out of the cylinders, the pressure would crack the pistons, and later they would come apart. I began to carry a spare cylinder, piston and gaskets with me.

The first time I changed a cylinder in a barnyard; I was young and didn't have a manual for the engine. I wasn't sure how to put it back together and time it. I was really surprised when I propped it, and it started and ran fine! I did not know then that, in the course of a few years, I would do this nine different times!

A friend of mine had a very nice Cessna 175 with a GO-300 engine. I always said the 175 Cessna was the "best airframe that Cessna ever built with the worst engine that Continental ever built!" The cylinders would crack and blow the heads off. My friend was a very good pilot and stayed very calm in exciting situations. The engine would blow a cylinder, and he always made a nice landing in a field.

He always asked me, "Lowell, will you replace the cylinder and fly it out for me?"

I did that five times and then told him, "Enough is enough!"

We had lost all confidence in the engine and I didn't want to want the sixth cylinder to blow. He sold the airplane that he liked so much, and only a few months later, Continental came out with a heavy cylinder which proved to be the answer to the problem. The new cylinders worked just fine.

On another occasion, I was riding with a friend of mine in his newly-purchased Aeronca Sedan, when, all of a sudden, a cylinder "blew off" and went right through the cowling. He turned the switch off and then did nothing. I looked over at him, and he was stiff and staring straight ahead. He had panicked and couldn't do anything. I turned the switch back on and took control of the airplane.

He kept saying, "You'll ruin the engine!"

I answered over and over, "The engine is ruined by the size of the hole in the cowling! We'd better try and save ourselves! We're over a lake and a swamp!"

I played with the throttle and, although it was popping and cracking, I was able to get 1500 RPM and 1800 RPM part of the time. I knew that an old Aeronca Sedan could fly just fine with this much power, and was able to make it to the airport safely. The engine was toast, but the plane was just fine. After we were on the ground for a while, the pilot started to feel much better. He continued to fly for many years.

On another occasion, I had picked up a Piper J-3 Cub just out of rebuild for a dealer. Flying home about half way across Illinois, the spinner bracket broke but didn't come off. With the spinner offset, everything was shaking so badly that I had to shut it down. Since it was just a Cub, it was easy to land in a field and remove the spinner. The flight home went just fine.

Another time I was flying a French Jodel-12 from southern Indiana for a dealer. Suddenly the vibration of the whole airplane was so bad that the plane looked twice as wide as it was. It was just a big blur! The Jodel uses a very long, pointed spinner and the backing plate had broken. The spinner turned sideways, throwing everything out of balance. The only available field was not real good. I did get down okay, with no damage.

I removed the spinner, and everything was running fine. However, I wondered how I was going to take off! With the help of some farmers who had watched me land, we managed to get the plane onto Highway 52. It wasn't easy, but once at the highway, the farmers blocked the road so I could take off.

Today, with better engines, better maintenance, and new rules, an engine failure is a rare thing! But they can happen from time to time.

.

PT-26

Back when I was picking up war surplus airplanes, I loved the PT-26's the best. In 1962 I found one that had blown its engine on takeoff. I was able to buy it and two other firewall forward PTs which included firewall, motor mount, engine cowling and nose bowl, and an extra prop for $1,250! As I searched for more parts, I noticed the plane had spent its entire life at Love Field in Dallas, Texas. I contacted the supply sergeant at Love Field.

"Boy! Are you in luck! I just got orders to clean out and junk all the PT parts! I've had them loaded in trucks, but just cannot bring myself to junk them yet!"

He told me he would send me everything I needed. Soon wooden boxes started showing up with all new parts for the engine, new wheels, many brake sets, tires and tubes, tail wheels, two new gas tanks, fuel pumps, many instruments, carburetors, master cylinders, throttles, mixture and carb heat controls. There was also a shiny, new brass wobble pump. You old "hangar rats know what that was and how it was used. All of this allowed me to rebuild the engine with all new parts!

The PTs were made mostly of wood, and since this one had sat outside after the engine had blown, the wings, center section, and tail assembly needed a lot of work. The wing spars and center section was constructed of Sitka Spruce while the covering was Birch plywood.

My PT had been built at Hagerstown, Maryland, but in 1942-43, they couldn't build enough of them so they were also built by Aeronca, St. Louis Street Car Company, and a lot of them were also built in Canada. The Hagerstown Museum wanted mine, since it was built in the original Fairchild factory.

I was about half finished with the rebuild, when money got real tight. We were always upkeeping extra kids who needed a lot of TLC, clothes, food, books, etc, so the project came to a halt. Then Art Eby, who owned a large Ford car and truck dealership, offered to supply the rest of the money to finish the plane as it should be.

As I was finishing the airplane, Art would spend his "day off" working on it too. The PTs used so many brass plates for service information, so Art took them all off and had them restored by a jeweler. They came back shining like gold! I installed them and coated them with clear coat. They are still shining today.

Art thought it would take us about sixty days to finish the rebuild, and my records show that it took 3 ½ years. During this time, Gay went to work as a secretary for Art. When it came time to paint the plane, Art said we should use the dealership's body shop. His painter was noted for fine paint jobs, and he said he would be glad to do the painting.

When the plane was finished, it was beautiful and flew like a dream! It took many awards over the years. We enjoyed many years of flying, but as time went Art wanted to upgrade to newer radios and newer NAV equipment. On top of that, the hangar rent, and insurance continued to go up. Besides that, the PT burned a lot of fuel. I could not justify my half of the expenses. Consequently, I sold my half to Art. Art was a great partner to share the plane with. and is still a good friend! I am thankful that I have had the pleasure to know him.

Art flew the PT for many more hours, until he wanted to move up to an AT-6 and then a T-34. He sold the PT, and I lost track of it until the original Fairchild Museum sent a picture and said they had acquired the PT. They usually had to restore planes to display, but mine looked so good they displayed it with our forty-year-old rebuild!

I wanted to go see it, but it was too far to go. Then we got a call to do an airworthiness inspection in Hagerstown, Maryland, and they would pay our expenses! We were on our way! But when we arrived, the museum door was locked. The airport manager said the building had been sold, and the planes were going for auction. We were heartbroken to hear that.

Ten years later, we received a newsletter from the Fairchild Museum. It turned out they had purchased land for a new building and outdoor display. They had been able to save the PT from auction! They hope to have the building finished soon.

I am very sentimental about this PT-26, because so much work went into it. I feel I have touched every single piece of this airplane and every single piece of that engine. It is great to see the PT lives on!

Too Big For Garage

People passing the Lowell Farrand residence on U.S. 33 east of Goshen in the past few days have noticed a rather unusual mode of transportation in his driveway. Farrand and Art Eby purchased a 1943 Fairchild PT-26 from a Granger resident and are now in the process of restoring the plane. The craft was built for the Canadian government and is powered by a 200 horsepower Ranger engine. The restoration work has been going on since the beginning of the year and Eby says they hope to have the plane completed in about 60 days. It will be housed at the Goshen Municipal Airport.

(Goshen News Photo)

Gay with the PT-26

Lowell in the Cockpit of the PT-26

Check out the museum's new website! Thank you to Ellen Green for her work on redesigning the website and upgrading the look and social media features. Many photos have been added in galleries that link to Flickr and videos link to YouTube. You can buy items in the gift shop and become a museum member or renew your membership on this website.

Also Like and Follow the museum's Facebook page. Currently 2242 friends of the museum like the page. This is a great way to reach a lot of people quickly with news, events and museum activities. The museum invites you to post your museum event photos and related local aviation photos to the Facebook page

News about the museum opening and their website. Lower right corner is "our" PT-26—still bringing pleasure to aviators from all around!

.

LOWELL FARRAND, DAR

DOING DAR INSPECTIONS

While I was still working at Economy Auto Supply, I was always also restoring airplanes. I tried to restore one plane each winter and sell it in the spring. This gave me money to fly my Luscombe. After I retired from Economy, I was able to spend more time rebuilding airplanes. I can figure I restored about fifteen airplanes over the years. After getting all that experience, I decided I would apply for the FAA DAR Inspection Program. I was accepted to take the course.

Gay and I traveled to Oklahoma City where I graduated as a DAR. To this date, Gay and I have inspected and issued 640 Airworthiness Certificates in six different classes of aircraft.

I have enjoyed the aircraft inspections very much. Sometimes the memories are about the airplane, and sometimes they are about the people. We have met so many wonderful people and always found out that people who complete aircraft projects are also great, dedicated people. I have always tried to make the inspection process a relaxing and enjoyable time. Some builders are so nervous and worried about their inspection, so I try to make it a celebration for them.

When I first started to inspect airplanes, many of the builders wanted me to make the first test flights. I had trained myself to come down and debrief as soon as possible after the test flight while I could still remember all the information about the trim of the airplane, its characteristics, and the temperatures and pressures of the engine. I had found that most builders are so excited about their airplanes, that they make the test flight, but they cannot remember the speeds, temperatures, etc.

While test flying experimental amateur built airplanes, I noticed the people that followed the plans the closest, their airplanes always flew the best. On doing inspections, we always had trouble with builders not following the plans. They always wanted to add something, or they wanted to "beef something up!" In doing so, they inadvertently added weight, and sometimes it caused dangerous conditions.

One of our best builders was a Brother of Holy Cross, Notre Dame. Brother Richard built a Mini-Max exactly according to the plans. He didn't change anything or add anything. I made the first test flight for him. It was in perfect trim and flew "hands off" for the first light. The engine temperatures were perfect, and there was nothing to change! That shows what a great job he did in building and also the great job that Wayne Ison did in designing, engineering and testing his kits. Just follow the plans, guys!

Flying "first flights" kind of became my reputation in the experimental airplane crowd. I have many memories of those first flights. Our EAA Chapter President, with the help of the chapter members, had built a very nice SONEX. I made his first test flight. I knew the TLC the guys had built into it, so I felt a special responsibility. My job was to test all the control inputs, the trim, and how well the plane flew. I was to also check all engine temperatures and pressures. While taxiing out, I noticed that the engine was idling too fast, so I had to drag the brakes.

The tower cleared me for takeoff, and, as I was climbing out, they called for a left turn out of the pattern. Just then the engine went rough and rich. I was trying to use the mixture control which was very sensitive while talking to the tower and trying to monitor all of the engine instruments. I asked the tower for permission to stay in the pattern so I could iron out some issues. The engine finally settled down nice and smooth, and the remainder of the test flight went very well. My emotions, on the other hand, were running fairly high!

On another test flight in a KR-II, things got kind of exciting. The preflight and taxi test went well, but on takeoff, just at lift off speed, the left brake locked up and turned me right toward a runway light! I pulled the plane off the ground, straddled the runway light, missed everything, and got the plane up into the air. I retracted the gear and flew out to a test area to check out all the maneuvers and trim. The engine was running well—all pressures and temperatures normal. I returned to land, and the gear wouldn't come down!

"Oh WOW! Now THIS!" I thought.

I worked the gear, shook the plane and bent the gear handle, but I got the gear down. I figured the brake had locked up because it got too hot. I flew around with the gear down, hoping to cool the brake. Not knowing if it would lock up on landing, I tried to land as slow as possible and was just rolling out then the left brake locked again!

I was able to keep it on the runway, though I zigzagged a bit. It turned out the brake drum was out of round and got hot spots which locked it up. With the landing gear retracted, the tires fit too tightly in the wings and locked up. It was a simple matter to fix and get more clearance for the wheels. The plane went on to fly very well for many years.

I really enjoyed first flights, but later Gay didn't want me to do them. So, as I got older, I quit making most of them—as far as Gay knows, but we won't tell her. Now I try to coach the builders about the characteristics of the airplane that they built also to remember the speeds, temperatures, etc. I tell them to plan for an emergency and have the plane well in their head before they make that first flight. I also try to arrange a flight in a plane that is the make and model of the one they have built.

One inspection I remember well was a beautifully built RV-6. The riveting and all of the construction was the most perfect I'd seen. The electronic instrument panel was the best wiring job ever. I found out the builder had been an Electronic and Mechanical engineer before he retired!

I inspected the entire airplane and found a bolt coming out of the lower connection of the control stick and the elevator push rod tube. The bolt had no nut on it and was too short. It had already worked itself halfway out. When I told him, he almost fainted! He was extremely upset.

"That's why I inspect everything before you fly!" I said calmly.

"You don't understand!" he said, "I was taxiing fast to check out the brakes, and it took off! So I had no choice but to fly around the field and land!"

He couldn't believe that the bolt stayed in. He said he remembered while building the plane that the bolt was too short to get a nut on it. He went to get the correct bolt, and the phone rang. After that, he forgot about the bolt. I told him that I always hope that I find any wrong bolts, missing nuts or cotter keys or safety wires. That is why it is always good to have an extra set of eyes to check the plane!

The DAR that had been inspecting the planes in Kentucky area was extremely well-liked and a great guy. Most of the pilots knew Pat, and he had told them he would inspect their projects when they were ready, but, sadly, he passed away unexpectedly. We started getting calls for inspections from all over Kentucky. I knew Pat well, so I told the guys I would do his inspections for them.

One day, while driving to an inspection in the Kentucky hills, our GPS took us on some very narrow, bumpy roads. The road we were on finally got down to two tracks. We called the builder on the cell phone.

"Stay right there! I'll come and find you!"

After a few minutes, here came a pickup. We followed him around hilly, curving turns, and he suddenly turned into a farm field and started up a hill. We came out on top of the hill, and there lay the most gorgeous green landing strip you could imagine. Beside it stood a beautiful log office building and a group of hangars.

The fellow had just finished a very nice RV-7 and also had the nicest Luscombe that I had ever seen—it really caught my eye. We had a very good inspection and a good time with the builder. It was starting to get dark, and I believed we needed to leave. My concern was how to find our way back to civilization. The roads back were very dark, but we made it.

At another inspection in Louisville, Kentucky, I needed to have a test area for him. It had to be away from congested areas. I applied to the FAA for the test area and they turned it down—too congested! I modified it away from most of the congested area, and FAA again turned it down—too congested. I then noticed a river close to the pattern and applied for the test area to be down the river to a clear area to do the testing and then using the river as a corridor turning up the river back to the airport. The FAA OK'd that one. It was a very nice RV-8. After some paperwork issues, we were able to issue his Airworthiness Certificate.

ONLY IN KENTUCKY!

Since I built the first Powered Parachute and tested it while working with Notre Dame Aero Space Division, I have always been interested in the PPC's and how far they have come. It seems like the same type of pilot that is attracted to the Powered Parachute is also interested in the Flexed-wing Trike type of aircraft. Usually when a group gets together for inspections, there would be about the same number of Trikes as PPC's.

A group from Kentucky called one day and had fifteen Trikes and fifteen PPC's ready to inspect. I told them to get them all together in one place, so two fellows got them together in a very large park. It turned out to be a very cold, windy day, and snow was predicted. I got half of them inspected, but it was too cold to do the paperwork in an open pavilion.

One of the older fellows said to me, "See that Catholic church up on the hill? I know the Father there. I'll ask if we can use a room there."

The Father provided us with a very nice, warm room to do the paper work in. He said he was sorry we couldn't use it the next day because they were having a big meeting there. We were able to get the last fifteen planes inspected the following day just as the big snow began. Again, we would need a place to do the paperwork.

Another fellow said, "Well, if the Catholics can give us a room, I'm calling my pastor and the Presbyterians can help us out too!"

He made a quick call to the pastor who said, "Come on down! The ladies are setting up for their bazaar, but we'll find you a room."

We drove in to the next town and went to the Presbyterian church to finish the paperwork. The ladies even kept us in coffee and cookies. It smelled so good in there!

The younger guys who had their PPC's and Trikes there for the inspection were all dressed in their hunting clothes and very anxious to go hunting from their aircraft right away. It was the first day of hunting season, and that is just like an important national holiday in those parts.

I looked up at them and asked, "Isn't it illegal to hunt from your aircraft?"

They all grinned sheepishly and replied, "In Kentucky, we make our own rules about hunting."

Another Kentucky inspection took place at Mt. Olivet. As we followed our GPS, the roads got smaller and smaller until we came to a very small bridge that looked homemade! We pulled over to decide what to do, when an old pickup truck whizzed past us and zipped across that bridge with the boards hopping up and down. We decided that if he could cross the bridge, then we could too.

We followed the road to the top of Mt. Olivet, where there was a house and a really nice shop/hangar. In front of the shop, there was a very short, but nicely mowed "apron" which immediately dropped over the cliff and down about four thousand feet! I inspected his aircraft, a very nicely built Kit Fox.

My curiosity got the best of me, so I asked, "You have such a nice shop and hangar, but where do you take off from?"

"Oh! Right here!" he pointed. "I just take off straight over the cliff! With the nose down, I pick up flying speed real quick! When I come in to land, I come up from below with full power, but right at stall speed and set the plane right in front of the hangar! I've flown here for years, and it's always worked!"

I shook my head and thought, *"Only in Kentucky."*

On another Kentucky inspection, Gay and I arrived at the airport gate and called the builder on his cell phone to ask him for the gate code.

"Aw, just drive close to the gate, and it will open," he said.

"I'm on the outside. I need to come IN," I said.

"Yep. Just drive up to the gate, and it will open," he repeated.

Again, I shook my head, *"Only in Kentucky!"*

We drove on in and met a really neat bunch of pilots/builders. On inspecting the airplane, I found the workmanship was very good, but in an area under the seat, I saw something that didn't look right. I used my inspection mirror and determined that it was some tools. I showed them what I had seen.

"OH! We've been looking all over for those! We turned this hangar upside down wondering where those tools got to!"

It was going to take some work and some riveting to remove the tools, but then all was well. I completed the inspection, and we said our goodbyes.

As we got ready to leave, the guys all said in unison, "You'll need a gate code to get out!"

"Isn't that a little backwards?"

"Aw no! We let everybody IN, but we want to talk to them awhile before they can LEAVE!"

Gay and I looked each other laughing. I whispered, "Only in Kentucky!"

ULTRALIGHTS

I became good friends with Wayne Ison while working at Notre Dame on the parafoil project which involved perfecting the parachute, and then the powered version of it. Wayne belonged to our EAA Chapter 132 and was marketing a homebuilt aircraft kit called PDQ2, which stood for Pretty Darn Quick. I helped him make up the kits, and I built the engines for them.

After the winter of 1978—The Great Blizzard— Wayne and his family left Elkhart, Indiana, and moved to Tulahoma, Tennessee. There were other aircraft designers from the Oshkosh, Wisconsin, area already settled there.

Wayne designed the Mini-Max. I really missed working with him in Elkhart. I became a dealer for the Mini-Max planes. In the first year, I had sold 24 complete kits. I later ended up with all of the prototypes to test and demonstrate them on my airstrip. Wayne and I made many trips to Oshkosh and to Sun 'n' Fun Fly-in in Lakeland, Florida to demonstrate, sell the plans, kits and airplanes.

I demonstrated the original prototype Two-Place TA-3. After several years, it was sold, and we had lost track of it. It was finally located by a neighbor, and he purchased it and restored it. It is now back at our airstrip again! The Mini-Max Company has sold several times, first to JDT Mini-Max, where I worked making up the kits. Then later it was sold to Team Mini-Max in Niles, Michigan. I am field representative for that company. Builders still call me with their questions.

I enjoyed the Ultralights, because now I could afford to fly and build airplanes. The Mini-Max also met the Ultralight rules, but flew like a heavier and bigger plane. It handled more wind than a "so-called" Ultralight. I traded a home-built for my first Mini-Max, because I didn't want to take the time to build it. I have built many of them since the start of the company, and I still get many calls and lots of questions.

Since China didn't have any small wooden airplanes, they sent their master woodworker to come to the factory to learn about building them. I got to show him all about building the Mini-Max. We built a set of wooden wings. The only two English words he knew were food and potty. We had a really good time. I took him flying and let him fly. He just couldn't believe our country, and was amazed that his motel room had a Bible in it! He appreciated his visit so much that he went home and created a working wooden watch for me. It is really beautiful, and he was quite the artist!

PLANES AND PEOPLE

While doing Airworthiness Inspections for aircraft, I found that the story of the people that built the aircraft is often more interesting than the airplane. All inspections are interesting. Sometimes it is about the construction of different types of airplanes, different engine installations, and sometimes it is about the people. Usually, it is both.

After 2010, FAA gave Ultralight and Two-place Ultralights a special waiver, and they had until 2010 to get them "grandfathered in" to the Experimental Light Sport Category. People began to call me from quite a distance in other states for inspections.

An instructor from Buffalo Ridge, Virginia, called and wanted an inspection. I told him that I wasn't sure we could afford to drive that far for an inspection.

"Oh, I have fifteen Powered Parachutes and seventeen Flex Wing Trikes at this field. I live nearby in Lynchburg, Virginia."

He was hoping we could come there and visit. What an answer to prayer! Buffalo Ridge had a very nice grass runway on top of the ridge, and a nice hangar and office for teaching. From the runway, all you could see in any direction was hills. For us Indiana "Flatlanders," taking off from that runway looked "kinda" scary! They do it all the time and think nothing of it.

We had a wonderful time getting to know each pilot and airplane. Our son Grant and his wife drove down to Lynchburg, and we had a great weekend with them, and Matt and a friend. We got the "grand tour" of Liberty University, walked on Liberty Mountain, and attended Thomas Road Baptist Church. What an awesome experience.

Buffalo Ridge called us again the next year with more aircraft to inspect. When we arrived, the instructor took us to his home for dinner. Turned out he and his wife met at Liberty University. They are both teachers, and their oldest son attended Liberty.

A Powered Parachute School instructor called from Detroit, Michigan, and said he had many PPC's, Flex Wing Trikes and a couple of other aircraft to be inspected and "grandfathered" into the Experimental

Light Sport Category at his home strip. He would make arrangements for us to stay at one of the pilots' homes. We were taken to a gorgeous home and stayed overnight. The next morning, a number of pilots joined us for breakfast there. The host and hostess were both detectives in Detroit and great cooks and story tellers. We spent two days inspecting, and the last evening at supper the hostess saw the pilots looking at the beautiful evening and said, "Go on, you guys go flying, and I'll hold dessert!"

Gay went with a Powered Parachute Pilot, and I went with another. We flew over the bay that came into Detroit from Canada, and we could see 100 year old ship wrecks in the bay and the red setting sun glowing in the buildings of Detroit. It was beautiful, but I was growing concerned about getting back to the grass strip since it was getting dark. I told the pilot we had a large four-engine airplane coming toward us, and it was close. I was in a real panic because it was so dark.

Just then, the pilot called the C-130, "Okay, light up our runway!"

The huge C-130, with flaps down and all his lights on, came down beside us and lit that runway better than daylight..

I said, "Wow! That's something when you can call a C-130 to light up your runway!"

"Oh, he's one of us. He flies a Powered Parachute too!"

The next day, while we were doing inspections, a "kid" who looked to be about fifteen came in wearing his "camo".

"Here's your C-130 pilot," one of the guys said.

Gay and I asked, "Did your mother drive you over here? You can't be old enough to drive—let alone fly!"

We finished the inspections and swapped many more stories. Each pilot had a story to go with their very nice aircraft.

Before Gay and I left, the instructor wanted to show us his grandfather's 100-year old car. It was a 1903 Sears and Roebuck kit car. He even had the catalogue that his grandfather ordered the car from and the receipt. It was a two-cylinder opposed engine that still runs great. They actually drive it in parades. Gay and I were lucky enough to drive it down the runway and back. It used a tiller bar instead of a steering wheel, and it drove very smoothly.

Near Detroit, Michigan. 1903 Sears and Roebuck Car out of the catalogue!

A Powered Parachute club called from Wisconsin and said they had many PPC's also needed to be inspected and "grandfathered" into the new Experimental Light Sport Category. This group made arrangements for us to stay at a very high class hotel. This group had fifteen or sixteen PPC's to be inspected and a few experimental airplanes. They had a very nice airport with a fully-equipped hangar/office. The walls were covered with beautiful pictures the pilots had taken in early morning sunrises and at sunset. Some were framed, and they also had videos of those flights for sale. Needless to say, they were breathtaking! We spent a wonderful two days meeting the pilots and inspecting their planes. On the last evening, the pilots and wives took us to an old coach house that was now a really neat restaurant. After a lot of story swapping, including those of the sheriff and a few state troopers, we went upstairs to their county historical museum. It contained a large collection of period clothing, old stage coaches and other memorabilia.

One day, we got a call from Romeo, Michigan, that a group at a small airstrip had about seventeen airplanes operating under the waver for two-placed ultralights and heavy ultralights. They too needed to be inspected and "grandfathered in" to the Experimental Light Sport category. Gay and I followed our GPS to the location, thinking, that way, it would be easier to find the next morning. We found the driveway and had driven a little way into the property to make sure we were at the right place. As we started backing out to go find a motel, the people saw us and waved us to come on in.

"We want you to stay with us!"

We all talked way into the night. The next day, the lady took Gay with her to church where she had some office work to do. Then they went shopping. I became very busy inspecting airplanes, most of which were Flight Stars and Phantoms. They caught my eye, because, at the time, I flew my own Flight Star. I was very interested in their Flight Star stories—the trips they had made, the different engines they had installed. All of the planes were very well-maintained.

The owner of the field was also a brilliant inventor. For example, he showed us his huge twelve-foot big wheel bicycle. He also invented two twelve-foot big wheels with a porch swing suspended between them. It was motorized so you could drive it around, which is exactly what Gay and I got to do!

Later that day, he got a call from his factory that a machine was down and needed immediate repair. He invited me along, and that factory was very interesting. The machine was a very large CNC machine that he had made, and it was programmed to make automobile bumpers. (Remember this was back when bumpers were still made of steel.)

They repaired the machine, because it was very important to keep it running 24 hours a day to keep up with the orders. The factory was huge, and all the machines, which were built or modified by him, were making parts—car and tractor parts—of the same material as the original. The paint was exactly the same as the original.

"Some of the older cars can be completely made from our parts bins!"

That evening the couple made supper for all the pilots and families so we could get better acquainted.

"Now," warned the Missus, "the grandkids are coming too, so watch your language! I know how pilots can get carried away!"

The next morning, as we gathered for breakfast, the host asked, "Can I share a story with you?"

We said, "Sure!"

"Well, about a year ago, I was diagnosed with a brain tumor. The doctors said it was inoperable. I went to the barbershop, and the guys asked how I was doing. So, I told them. One of the guys asked if he could pray for me. And I told him, 'Sure'. The next week when I went for my check up, the doctors could find no sign of any tumor! Praise the Lord!"

There are simply times we can say without a doubt that:

"the Sun of Righteousness shall arise with healing in
His wings."
Malachi 4:2.

This was one of them.

As I said earlier, sometimes it is all about the airplanes, and sometimes it is all about the people. Most of the time it's the people and their airplanes, and it is good.

5 BROTHERS, LLC

We received a call to inspect an RV-12 Experimental Light Sport Airplane. At first, I hesitated as the plane was located on the Ohio/Pennsylvania border. It was quite a way to go for only one inspection. However, they sounded so nice—I just couldn't say no!

When we arrived, we were met by the most wonderful people. Even their license plate told us they were Christians! He was an airline pilot, and their oldest daughter had just received her private pilot license the day before. We then met the other four pilot/builders. All five of them had formed "The 5 Brothers, LLC" to build the RV-12.

The airplane was beautifully built, and the inspection went very well. They were quite excited as we took pictures of them receiving their Airworthiness Certificate for the plane. While doing the inspection, I, a Breezy caught my eye. I had done an annual inspection for a Breezy at our home air strip for twenty-seven years. After each annual, I would fly it for one hour.

I commented on how beautiful their Breezy was, and they asked if we would like to see the area from it! Gay got to see the beautiful Amish farms with shocks of corn and wheat—all hand-harvested. Then I got to see the area at about 100 feet! Oh! It was beautiful! He said his wife—also a pilot—and their two daughters all loved the Breezy, along with sail planes and, of course the RV-12.

A few months later his oldest daughter finished her training to be an FAA Traffic Controller. It wasn't long after that she recognized her father's voice on the radio and was able to direct his airline flight!

So many memories come to mind about the builders of aircraft. Anyone that has the skills to build a beautiful airplane also has skills in other things. One builder of an RV-6 builds nice quilt frames that he sells all over the country. His wife has won many honors with her quilts, and she sells many of them and displays others in museums. A fellow had wanted to buy one she had hanging on the wall. He offered her five thousand dollars, and she said NO. It was a complete farm scene with barns, fields and crops. She even embroidered the corn stalks in the foreground.

Another fellow cleared a wooded area, cut trees down and had them sawed for lumber to build the house he and his wife had designed. They had porches that overlooked a pond and wild life. Another built a nice J-3 Cub replica. He did a wonderful job building everything himself. He builds organs for a living, cabinets and all. We saw several of them and he played beautiful music on them. I am always so amazed at the talent and skills that people have. They don't just build an airplane either—they craft it. They are true artisans.

Serenade to a Homebuilder

My Husband has a hobby
which really keeps him busy.
The activity in our garage
often makes me dizzy!

I always know where he is…
after work, evenings and weekends too!
With this project there's
always something to do.

He's working on the gas tank,
the frame, and wings are done.
He pounds, shapes, drills and

welds—his idea of fun.

He stands back, admires his work,
and in his mind sees himself soar.
He tilts his head, listens, and
I know he hears his engine roar.

He has become an artist in
his own way
Carefully planning for that
one great day.

And on that one great day
he will head for the sky
And I will be with him
ready to fly

Author unknown

Lowell presenting Airworthiness certificate to the 5
Brothers LLC

Lowell and Gay with a "Brother" and the Breezy

OUR LITTLE "SLICE OF HEAVEN"

Back in 1975, I had the idea to find a place for an airstrip where I could also build a house. A friend told me about a grass strip and that maybe the farmer would sell me a lot. Sure enough, he agreed, and, in the fall of 1976 we had two hangars full of an airplane and furniture that was ready to go in the house as soon as it was finished. (I am sure you can see the priorities here, correct?)

Gay had drawn up the blueprints for the house, and we went to the bank for a loan. She wasn't sure the plans were good enough, but they assured us that they were better than a lot of those the contractors brought in! It was plans for a small cozy A-frame structure.

Later, Gay's grandmother climbed the spiral staircase to the loft and said, "It's made just like a hog shed!"

Later on, we added a greenhouse and a hot tub. There were planes in the farmer's building, and then another fellow bought a lot next to us and put up a hangar! So we had more planes and pilots! We were excited about that.

One morning about 5:30 am, as Gay was eating breakfast, she heard a loud engine. She ran outdoors in time to see a crop duster swoop very low over our house! Even now, many years later, we run out every time we hear an airplane fly over. The Med-Evac helicopter makes flights from the Goshen Airport to Fort Wayne Hospitals going right over our back porch and hangars. We always stop and pray for the passenger and crew.

We have given many kids their first airplane ride from this airstrip. One summer a large home-school group contacted us about EAA Young Eagles flights. We lined up several planes, including a four-place one. We flew from 8 am until 6 pm, and even flew a couple of parents and grandparents. We went through a lot of cookies, iced tea, Kool-aid and coffee that day. It was wonderful!

We have had several people stop on their way home from the big Air Venture fly-in at Oshkosh, Wisconsin. One was a young girl in a Luscombe from California who left here and went to the East Coast and then back home. Another couple of fellows stopped and stayed over for several days, and we showed them "Amish country" and other features of our area.

Since our retirement, we have lots of folks stopping in—to talk, ask questions about their airplanes, borrow tools, and more. It's a great way to meet people. The "regulars" know we'll always have cookies and coffee or iced tea. One of the fellows who keeps a plane in the farm hangar shared his life story with me, and then I shared mine. He asked me to share it at his church. We have become close friends with him, and his wife and now attend the same church, where there are several other pilots!

A few years ago, we added on to the house, and sadly the hot tub "gave up the ghost". We do miss it!

For several summers we enjoyed having Amish men and boys flying their RC planes at the strip. It was amazing to see the expertise they had with their planes. There were never any crashes. Sometimes the whole family came and brought picnic lunches for everyone or ordered pizza delivery for everybody. They even threw a surprise birthday party for one of the boys. They also loved driving the golf cart!

In recent years, there is a group of pilots that have cookouts here at the hangar. Two ladies cook on the grill and everybody brings something to share. We have plenty of food and fun and flying—all in one great evening. It doesn't get much better than that here on this earth!

Two other drop-ins actually came just in time to save my life. A car drove up and dropped off two large, wild cats down near the hangars. A few days later I could see that they had been staying in our second hangar. One was a large golden cat, and one was a grey tiger. I tried to pet them, but they would just run and hide. If I got too close, they would hiss at me.

I started putting kitty food and milk out for them every day. By the next morning, it would be all gone. I began to notice that I never saw a mouse in any of the hangars since they arrived. So, I thought—if they get the mice, I'll keep feeding them. This went on for about a year. Then, one cold, winter morning we had about six inches of snow and the temperature was four below! I wasn't happy about having to go out and feed the cats. As I bent over to fill their dishes, I wondered why the lights were getting so dim in the hangar.

Much later, I woke up, face down on the floor, and one of the cats was lying over my neck and the other cat was licking my forehead. I couldn't move for quite a while. I figured Gay wouldn't come out to the hangar, as she probably thought I was working on some project. My legs wouldn't work, so I used my elbows to crawl through the six inches of snow, and then I banged on the back door.

After she got me inside, I told her I should probably get checked out at the hospital. She called Lavern, our neighbor, and he took us to the hospital.

The ER Doctor said, "You're going to get a pacemaker!"

I had had a heart rhythm problem, and had worn a monitor several times, but it didn't show any problem. The doctor then said something that really shocked us.

"Those cats saved your life by keeping your blood warm, otherwise, you would have had a stroke!"

After the surgery, and I recovered, I went out to feed those wild cats, but they wound around my legs so much I could hardly walk. They licked me all the way to their dishes! After that, they needed petting before I could put food in their dishes.

Everyone called them, Lowell's "Angel Kitties"! Several years later, they disappeared on their own, but we have seen little gold kittens and little tiger cats around our neighborhood from time to time ever since.

God DOES give His angels charge over us, doesn't He? His words even say so:

> *He will give His angels charge concerning you.*
> *To guard you in all your ways.*

Psalm 91:11

Our house and the strip from a Meyers OTW biplane.
The Meyers Company made this model of biplane to win
the trainer competition. The OTW means "Out to Win,"
but, sadly, they didn't.

The Monument: Some of Lowell's buddies did this for
him. The party was to be a cookout for these buddies,
and their wives. Boy, were we fooled!
Steve Linton (Linton Monument Co)
Bernie Yoder
Don Duck, Sr.
Terry Batchelor
Bill Weaver
And so many others!

AFTER THOUGHTS

It's too bad that I can't write a book about the feelings, emotions, smells and sounds of an aircraft starting up. The smell of AV-gas and a puff of smoke from 100 weight oil as a big round engine starts and warms up—there's nothing like it! I've always wished that I could spill some AV-gas on a page of the book and cover it with that 100-weight oil and paint it over with fabric and airplane "dope"!

I would add a "chip" on the page to play the sound of that radial engine starting up, so you, dear reader, could have the real experience like I've had so many times. Gay used to say when we were dating, that if she could use AV-gas for cologne and 100-weight oil for hand cream, and fabric dipped in aircraft dope for her hankie, and then I would be really happy!

I wish I could write in a book the emotions of all my first flights, when testing a new airplane or first flights in experimental airplanes. Or I could write the emotions of the summer we got the B-29 and the PT Boat on the Government Bidders List! We were so excited at first and then it turned to utter despair when we found out the cost and all the Government Regulations that we were faced with. A whole summer was lost in despair, and our nerves were just "shot". Our parents were mad at us; our friends were scared that we might beg for money. We had no idea how we would get out of that mess. Then we prayed. And God sent us some good people who helped us out of our dilemma.

Maybe the story written on these pages can give you some idea of the depths of my emotions. I hope so.

Note from Becky: "Well, I say you <u>have</u> written such a book! I have certainly felt the depths of your experiences, and you and Gay are forever written in my heart. It's been a joy putting this together with you, and I have laughed and cried with you, feeling every story as if I were there." Rebecca McLendon

ACKNOWLEDGEMENTS

I just want to give thanks for GOD'S gift of my life. HE has given me my wife and wonderful family. He has given us countless friends along the way. Also, thanks to HIM for saving me so many times when my judgment was so poor that I could have lost my life without HIS hands on me. Thanks, Lord for my life. YOU are an AWESOME GOD!

Those whose hope is in the LORD
will renew their strength,
they will soar on wings like eagles;
they will run & not grow weary,
they will walk & not faint.
IS 40:31

43162130R00117

Made in the USA
Middletown, DE
22 April 2019